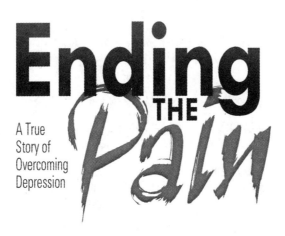

Ending THE Pain

A True
Story of
Overcoming
Depression

LINDSEY GENDKE

Pacific Press®
Publishing Association
Nampa, Idaho | Oshawa, Ontario, Canada
www.pacificpress.com

Cover design by Steve Lanto
Cover design resources from iStockphoto.com
Interior design by Aaron Troia

The author assumes full responsibility for the accuracy of all facts and quotations as cited in this book.

You can obtain additional copies of this book by calling toll-free 1-800-765-6955 or by visiting http://www.adventistbookcenter.com.

Library of Congress Cataloging-in-Publication Data

Gendke, Lindsey, 1984-
    Ending the pain : a true story of overcoming depression / Lindsey Gendke.
    Nampa : Pacific Press Publishing, 2016.
    ISBN 9780816361144 (pbk.)
 1. Gendke, Lindsey, 1984-   2. Depressed persons—Religious life.
3. Depression, Mental—Religious aspects—Christianity.
    4. Suicide—Religious aspects—Christianity.
    BV4910.34.G46 2016
    248.8/625—dc23

February 2016

We don't just have stories; we are a story. It is our responsibility to know our story so we can live it out more intentionally and boldly for the Great Story, the gospel. God writes our story not just for our own enlightenment and insight but to enlighten others and to reveal His own story through our story.

— **Dan Allender**, *To Be Told*[1]

1. Dan Allender, *To Be Told: God Invites You to Coauthor Your Future* (Colorado Springs: Westbrook Press, 1999), 51, 52.

Dedication

For Buc—God sent you when I needed you, and I will always be grateful. Thanks for inviting me into your life and showing me about God's love by giving me your own.

Contents

Disclaimer

Anytime an author writes nonfiction about her personal life, other lives are involved. While I wrote some painful, potentially embarrassing scenes, it was not my goal to bring pain to any party, but to shed light on the causes, extent, and results of my depression, and to ultimately help others. For those "characters" who were most intimately and vulnerably involved (immediate family; close, current friends), I got permission to share what I did. For some other characters who I am not in contact with (such as ex-boyfriends), I have changed names to protect privacy.

Like all writers, I had to make many choices about what to keep and what to cut. Out of consideration for the reader, I sometimes compressed multiple conversations into single scenes, and for the sake of a tight narrative, I enhanced certain moments and details that served my message, while downplaying or excluding others that did not.

Regarding accuracy: though my "characters" may remember things differently, I wrote each scene and each chapter to the best of *my* memory, checking fuzzy details in my journal or with involved parties when I could, and/or when complete and total accuracy was important. While I certainly don't remember each word that was spoken, my goal with my dialogue was to preserve the spirit of the conversations, so the reader would have the same *sense* of the moment that I hold in my memory.

Prologue

I can never tell, I thought, sitting in a mental ward in Minnesota.
I was nineteen.

When I get out, I can't tell friends that I dropped out of college. That I, a "Christian," attempted suicide. I can't tell them how messed up I am or how messed up my family is. I can't let them see me like this.

When I got out after forty days, there was only one option . . . besides suicide, of course. I had to hide.

My social worker set me up in an efficiency apartment that was fully furnished and yet covered in grime. The walls were spotted with grease stains, the floors covered in dirt. *Kind of like me.*

Only, instead of dirt, I was filthy with lies—and they were rooted *deep.*

And unlike the dirt that disappeared in one afternoon's scrubbing, it would take me many, many years to recover from the lies that had saturated my mind for so long. It would take a redefining of faith, Jesus, and prayer.

I can never tell, I thought ten years later, before I realized that was also a lie. How could I be so selfish to keep this story in, when telling it to a few trusted others was what paved the way for healing?

Truth broke through. *Someone else needs this story, and my example of telling it, and the permission to be honest.*

So I offer my story of depression and healing—and, more important, my story of learning to replace Satan's lies with God's truth. The truth is, Jesus suffered and died for me because I was worth it to Him, even when I wanted—and tried—to throw my life away.

Part 1—Bad Roots

Healing is a long process. After a stressful childhood that slowly builds layers and layers of hurt, healing requires its own string of years to unfurl all those thickly laid wounds.

I'm inclined to think that wounds in childhood or adolescence might be harder to overcome, because that's when—so they say—people are busy building identities. If you get thrown off track just when you're supposed to be getting your bearings in life, or even before you really get your bearings, isn't it a little harder to find your true identity? Because, rather than returning to a place you've already come to know in life, you have to try to find a path you've never actually seen.

I feel like this was a large part of my post-depression struggle. The more I've pondered my "coming into my own" over the last few years, I feel like perhaps what I was trying to do was forge a person, an identity, I'd never really known. I wanted to be a happy, healthy, positive, goal-driven person. But I often had the sense that to become this person was to become something that was totally foreign. I was sad, wounded, and negative for so long that even if I was a positive person at one time, I just couldn't remember.

—from my "Writing to My Roots" notebooks, October 2012

Chapter 1

Desperate

Fall 2003

Lie: I have nothing to live for.

Several days before I attempted suicide, I stood in a church in Saint Cloud, Minnesota, surrounded by a sea of young adults with upraised hands and swaying bodies. I was at a revival for college students, and I was desperate. That's why I'd accepted this invitation from Rebekah and Easton, two seniors, Christians, who had been after my soul for weeks. They'd seen me walking past their Christian booth—perhaps they saw the quiet desperation in my eyes—and invited me to their Wednesday night praise group, and this event.

Outside of this, and the single Wednesday night I'd humored Rebekah and Easton, I wasn't attending church at all. I hadn't since age sixteen, when I left the Seventh-day Adventist Church. My college was Lutheran, but lots of students weren't religious at all. As I stood among the maze of spiritual seekers in Saint Cloud, I teetered on the brink of "not at all," but I was willing to be won over if Christianity really had anything to offer me.

I couldn't help but stare as a drummer and two guitarists banged out praise music from the stage, bodies swayed, and hands waved in the air. I felt like an anthropologist in a foreign country. My former church didn't worship like this. They didn't play drums in the sanctuary, and they never put their hands up like that.

"I could sing of your love forever," the singers sang, and the audience echoed, over and over again, almost in raptures. The people kept repeating that one line: "I could sing of your love forever, I could sing of your love forever, I could sing of your love forever . . ." until they seemed in a trance.

I tried to hide my disbelief at the frenzy building around me. Ostensibly, we were all here for a "revival," but I doubted any of these celebrators needed reviving like I did. I wasn't here for a party, or a little encouragement, or a break from homework. I desperately needed saving.

But no one was paying attention to me. Everyone, including Rebekah and

Easton, was swaying, lifting hands, closing eyes, clutching hearts. I couldn't make myself do it. *Give me something to celebrate,* I mentally dared these people.

"We're here to be revived!" the keynote speaker exclaimed, tall and imposing as he took center stage. "Glory, oh, praise Jesus!"

The audience echoed.

"We're here to renounce the devil and claim Jesus in our lives. It doesn't matter who you are or where you come from, you have a new life in Christ from this moment on!"

"Glory, glory!"

"God has a plan for you. We are God's sons and daughters. But the devil, he wants to steal and kill and destroy that plan. He wants to get inside your heads and take all that away. He tells us lies: *I'm no good; God can't forgive me; my family has a history of mental illness, so I will suffer mental illness too.* But by the power of the Holy Spirit, those lies have no power over us! Amen!"

"Amen! Amen!"

"Yes, Lord!"

What? My head spun. I'd heard about "new life in Christ" before. I'd heard about Satan's lies, and the Holy Spirit. But even so, I didn't speak this language. I didn't know anything about new life in Christ. I only knew about depression and broken families and a dying will to live.

"We denounce those lies in our lives, and they have no power over us anymore. We rebuke the devil, and we claim the Holy Spirit, and we are made new!"

But how? My mind screamed. *How can I be made new?*

* * * * *

For years I'd looked forward to the new start college promised. No more family trouble, no more boyfriend trouble, no more depression. But at two and a half months in, I was failing at even the most basic things of college life—like the new "family" I was supposed to be part of.

At the beginning of the school year, the college had organized us freshmen into "family groups" led by capable upperclassmen. We'd spent our first week together, playing mixer games and getting oriented on campus. And these organized functions I had no trouble with; prescribed structure was easy. But now, our purely social meetings, our outings for ice cream and hamburgers, were hard. Even worse was finding people to eat lunch with or hanging out with the girls in my dorm. I didn't know how to belong in happy families. Once upon a time I'd had one of those, but it was almost before I could remember.

Indeed, I wasn't used to making friends or getting close to people; the ability to express myself freely and safely in groups had not been part of my normal experience for years.

Still, I hoped to be free and safe with at least one person, so, while the other freshmen spent hours getting to know one another, I spent hours on the phone with Chad, my new boyfriend, who had shown up during the lonely summer leading up to college.

The closest person I had at college was my roommate, Megan, whom the college had paired me with. But after just the first day, I concluded the match was a mistake. I have a picture of us together from move-in day, standing in the midst of unpacked boxes in our new room. There's Megan, tall and smiley in her aqua tank top and cascading bronze hair, draping a skinny, unabashed arm around my shoulders. And then there's me, pale and pudgy, trying to smile as I shrink my five feet, five inches under Megan's arm, hands bunched into baggy overalls that cannot hide the ten pounds I gained over the summer—my early start on the freshman fifteen—and my thick, golden hair pulled back into an embarrassed ponytail. Megan loved the camera, and I wanted to hide—and that's the difference between Megan and me.

From day one, Megan was meeting people and making friends. It was nothing for her to walk up to someone and say, "Hi, I'm Megan. What's your name?" and start up a conversation that could last through the next meal and beyond. She seemed happiest surrounded by a group of people, traveling around campus in a pack. At night she brought new acquaintances back to the room or stayed out late with the girls on the floor. She always invited me to go with them: "Hey, we're all watching *Friends* downstairs, you wanna come?" but I declined. I felt too awkward, like a puzzle piece trying to fit into the wrong picture.

Instead of getting to know my floor-mates, I camped in my room and journaled, or I called Chad. Instead of introducing myself to people in the caf, I sat by myself. I felt miserable, but I didn't want company. Sometimes I ran late at night, while other students studied or partied. Whenever I left late in workout clothes and tennis shoes, Megan gave me strange looks. She would never do anything like that. She had no need for a dark sky under which to hide.

But I did. Something was happening inside of me. I felt myself withdrawing more every day . . . from Megan, from Chad, from classwork, from the idea of life itself. *I could just end the pain right now*, a voice whispered every day in my ear. But I tried to push it away.

One night a few weeks into the semester, Megan and I lay sprawled on our loft beds, heads just feet apart. I was trying to journal, but she kept jabbering on and on about classes and new friends and the gigantic selection of food in the cafeteria and how, one day, she had just looked out the window and decided the world was a beautiful place.

"Um-hmm," I kept saying, trying to look interested. I hoped she would get the hint and stop talking.

"So, Lindsey," she said, flipping her shimmery hair over her shoulder, "How are you liking it here? What types of people are you meeting? How are you enjoying the college experience?"

My eyebrows shot up in surprise. For the first time in twenty minutes, Megan was completely silent and looking straight at me.

I searched my thoughts for some response I could give. *I hate this place. I hate my life. I don't want to meet people. I don't want to do anything. Life seems hopeless.* I chose the only acceptable answer: "Well, I'm still getting used to it."

Megan waited a moment more and then responded, "Well, I hope everything's OK. I've noticed you don't seem too happy."

Try suicidal, I thought.

"I'm happy to listen if you need to talk about anything."

Inwardly, I snorted. It was a nice offer, but I was sure her ears weren't big enough to handle everything I needed to talk about.

No one's ears are big enough to handle my *problems,* I thought.

"I appreciate your offer, but it's not a big deal. I have a little history with depression, and recently I stopped my medication." With my psychiatrist's consent, I had tapered off my Zoloft during the month of August.

"I think I'm just having some withdrawals," I said, shrugging. "I think it'll just take a little time for my system to get back on track."

I didn't mention that I couldn't even fathom what "on track" meant for me. When was the last time my life had been on track?

"Oh." Megan nodded. "I totally know what you're talking about."

Wanna bet? I thought. I raised skeptical eyebrows.

Megan said she had a history with depression too. But what she called "depression" sounded no worse than PMS. I couldn't relate to the experiences she described. She told me that whenever her mood began to deteriorate, she would give herself a "pep talk": "Come on, Megan, snap out of it." One time she spilled her guts to a counselor, only to hear at the end of the hour, "I can't really help you—you sound like you're already working it out." She said she could go to a psychiatrist feeling awful and at the end of a session be "all better." The apex of her condition came one time after two weeks of the blues. Sitting in the bathtub she cried out, "God, if I can't help myself, how can I help anyone else?" Suddenly, she said, she felt peace. It was a deeply spiritual experience. And she'd been happy ever since.

I kept waiting for her to mention the quandary about wanting to die, the question of life's meaning, and suicidal thoughts or attempts, but she never got there. And as she talked on and on about "overcoming depression," I decided she knew nothing about the subject.

Sadly, neither did I.

Through the next days and weeks and the falling leaves of autumn, I tried to let Megan's zest for life inspire me; but the harder I tried to keep up with her, the further behind I fell. Instead of feeling encouraged, I felt drained.

I'm so screwed up, I wrote on pages I planned to show no one. Who could ever understand? *I'll never be happy. I have no future, except this dismal depression.*

One late night when I staggered in from a run, Megan looked up in alarm. "Honey, are you *OK?*"

I flopped to the floor and tugged off my shoes. "Sure."

She didn't look like she believed me.

"What were you doing out running this late? You know I would've gone with you, don't you? You know you don't have to go alone."

I half smiled. "I know, thanks," I said. But I knew full well that I would never ask her to come with me; I knew full well that there was no other way than for me to go it alone.

Chad broke up with me in early October, and from there, I faded fast.

Thoughts of quitting college turned to thoughts of quitting life. I decided that if God didn't do something drastic, I would. And so, at nineteen, I found myself at a revival meeting without hope, except for one: maybe God would show up to talk me out of killing myself.

* * * * *

All around me, young men and women moaned, "Oh, Jesus, thank You, Jesus," as if mighty burdens were being lifted. But inside, all I felt was confusion and growing despair. Nothing the speaker said resonated with me except those negative thoughts that he said were Satan's lies. The "lies" sounded exactly like the thoughts in my head, but I could not denounce them because they weren't really lies: in my clouded understanding, they were *who I was,* and who I had been for the past five years.

How could he tell me to simply deny the "truth" I'd lived with for so many years and be free, right here and right now? How could he tell me I had a "new life," when a quick body check told me I was still the same miserable girl who had stepped into this church? I was still the girl with no "home," the girl who'd been dumped, the girl who couldn't muster a reason or a will to live.

I left feeling worse than when I'd come.

When our bus returned to campus, I headed to the basement of Pitts Hall, turned on one of the thirteen desktop computers, and opened a blank document.

"To everyone who has ever loved me . . ." I typed, relief cascading through my body.

All around me, my college-mates wrote essays, emailed professors, chatted online with friends back home . . . while I slowly, thoughtfully drafted my suicide note.

One hour later, I printed the document and went upstairs. The next day I would withdraw from college. I would make the arrangements and buy the supplies. And finally, I would end the pain. If God had other plans—if there even was a God—He'd have to intervene; as of that day, I was done trying at this game of faith and this game of life.

Chapter 2

Playing the Game

1990s

Lie: Following God is no fun.

*E*ven from a young age, I decided that for faith to make sense, it had to make a difference in my life—a *good* difference. I didn't care if what my family followed was "right"; I mostly wanted to see how our religion could make my life better. From what I could tell at age seven, it wasn't making my life better.

I hated almost everything about our so-called faith, starting with the fact that I had to wear dresses to church. My memories of early childhood are fuzzy, but I still feel strongly the negative emotions connected with Saturdays—the day on which we, as Seventh-day Adventists, worshiped. I still remember negative sounds, images, and feelings. I remember the constant conflict in our house and the rejection I felt at school. I remember wishing I could live somewhere else, go to a different church . . . even have a different family sometimes.

I'm sure it wasn't as bad as I made it out to be, but here's the thing: Even before life got really hard, I was melancholy. Even before I questioned my faith, or my family broke up, or multiple boyfriends broke up with *me,* I exemplified that "perfect melancholy"[1] personality that is simply prone to get depressed no matter whether life is rosy, no matter whether your mom makes home-cooked meals and tucks you in at night, no matter whether your dad teaches you softball in your front yard and volleyball in your backyard. True story, by the way. Those were my parents—wonderful, caring, loving parents who did the best they could with the knowledge and resources they had—and that was me. I was that very blessed but very melancholy child who saw the negatives in everything.

For melancholy types[1] who have not submitted their lives to God's control (and I did not submit until adulthood), the primary question is not *Will I get depressed?* but *What will I be depressed about?*

* * * * *

Bass notes, synthesizers, and Amy Grant's alto voice drifted through the sheet that covered my doorway. I winced, pulling my blankets over my head. It was starting again. This was how every Saturday morning started. Just like light after complete blackness hurts the eyes, the drums from the cassette tape hurt my ears, drove me deeper beneath the four-deep pile of covers that substituted for central heating. Dad's Sabbath music.

I smelled coffee, turkey bacon, and waffles. Dad's cooking.

Then Dad's head appeared, a dot on the side of the sheet.

"*Goo-ood* morning!" he sang out, blue eyes twinkling. "Breakfast is almost ready! Time to get up for church!"

"Ugh! I don't want to go!" I spat into my pillow, but Dad was gone.

If he wants me to go, he can make me, I thought, and snuggled deeper into my covers.

"Go and see why Lindsey isn't up," I heard several minutes later.

Miniature "Dad" appeared—my nine-year-old brother, Kyle. Both had showered and combed their sandy, tidy haircuts, dressed in khakis and polo shirts.

"Get up!" Kyle barked. "You're going to make us late!"

"I want Mom," I whined. I wanted Mom's soft hand stroking my forehead, lulling me out of sleep. I wanted her whisper-thin voice breathing, "Lambie," into my ear. I wanted things to be normal.

Kyle's jaw tightened. "She's not here. Get dressed. You better get in the kitchen, or Dad will spank you."

I made faces at the sheet wobbling in his wake. I scowled at the four bare walls enclosing me. They looked uglier than usual this morning. The crack between the floor and the wall seemed wider. The draft tickling my bare toes felt cooler. Winter was coming, and then what would we do? I already had to sleep with a pile of blankets to keep warm. Usually it was Mom who tucked me in, adding yet one more blanket when I told her, "I'm still cold, Mom." She piled on the blankets, tucking each one so tight I could barely move. I was still cold, but she said the weight would eventually turn to heat. Then, good English major that she was, she read to me: *Curious George, Amelia Bedelia, The Berenstain Bears.*

Lately I'd graduated to Beverly Cleary's *Beezus and Ramona.* I was learning to read for myself now, but I preferred to have Mom read. *Everything is better with her around,* I thought as I struggled into hot pink pants and a flowered shirt—the outfit I wore to school most days because I was so picky about clothes.

Every time Mom took me shopping it was an ordeal, trying to find blouses that fit right; pants were worse. Even socks were tough; if the seam bulged too much or rubbed my toes the wrong way, I wouldn't wear them. Mom told of a tantrum I threw at a neighbor's house when I was four because I didn't like my socks. She compared me to the princess and the pea. I didn't deal well with change. And a lot had changed recently.

"Dad, she's not dressed right," Kyle said, looking up from his plate of waffles.

"Shut up! It's none of your business!" He was always tattling on me. *Like he's so good,* I thought. In my eyes, Kyle was a bully who often took advantage of the two and a half years he had on me.

I knew the fight that would ensue, because it was the one we fought every Saturday: they would force me to wear a dress, and I'd resist until I couldn't any longer.

"Nobody at school wears a dress to *their* church."

"So help me . . ." Dad said, swatting at my behind, shooing me back to my bedroom. "Your mother should be here." He looked angry.

"But she's in the hospital, Dad. Didn't you say she's sick?" I tried to distract him.

"Yeah," he muttered. "She is." He pulled a dress off the hanger, which hung on nothing but a naked pole jutting down from my ceiling.

"Why do we have to go anyway, Dad? None of the other kids go on Saturday; it would be so much easier if we just went on Sunday like the rest of them."

The veins on his neck bulged. He struggled to pull the dress over my skinny frame.

"Tell me about it," he grunted. "We go on Saturday because it is the Sabbath. The Bible says to." His voice was even angrier now. He was tugging on my shoes. "We're . . . following . . . God," he spat, one word per tug. Finally the shoes were on. Dad was livid.

"Aren't we going to be late?" Kyle interjected, reappearing in my doorway.

"I hate dresses," I whined.

"Get in the car!" Dad yelled. "Now!" He juggled a plastic coffee cup and his Bible.

"I hate the Sabbath too," I pouted under my breath.

"Why do you have to ruin every Sabbath?" Kyle said as he took shotgun, while I climbed into the backseat. "You're such a baby. All you ever do is whine!" I lunged at him, but he flinched out of reach.

I cried the entire twenty miles to church.

* * * * *

That day, I was the only kid in Kindergarten. All the other kids were in different classes: the babies and toddlers in Cradle Roll, the second- and third-graders in Primary, and the fourth- and fifth-graders in Juniors. Not one of them, except Kyle, went to my school. Instead, they came from surrounding small towns like we did, because in Minnesota, unlike Catholic or Lutheran churches, Seventh-day Adventist churches weren't found just anywhere. Most of the kids at school and most of my cousins went to the same Lutheran church where Dad had been confirmed years before. They got cookies after church in the basement, and they got summer vacations from Sunday School.

But *Sabbath* School went all year round. I *never* got a break.

I sighed, slumping in my seat.

"How is Lindsey today?" the teacher asked.

"Fine," I said, crossing my arms and pretending—just like my parents, who greeted everyone with smiles as they walked in the door, even if minutes before they'd been yelling.

"Today's lesson is about the Sabbath. Remember how we've been studying the seven days of Creation? And how God rested on the seventh day?"

Of course I knew. How could I forget? It was all Seventh-day Adventists ever talked about. I knew we worshiped on the Sabbath because God *rested* on the Sabbath. This was the same day, my parents learned as searching Christians, that God commanded His followers to keep holy in the Ten Commandments—in fact, it was the only commandment Seventh-day Adventists proudly explained that God said to "remember," yet this was the one commandment most of the Christian world "forgot" to keep.

When Kyle and I were babies in Fargo, my parents, newly sprung from college and unmoored from their respective Minnesotan churches (Lutheran for Dad, Catholic for Mom), were invited by one of Dad's coworkers to attend a Revelation Seminar. After my parents attended the prophecy seminar, they couldn't argue with the Adventists. Their eyes had been opened to the truth, and they joined the church. Mom got baptized right away, but Dad would wait another decade until he felt more comfortable with the idea.

Now, Mom and Dad took us to church every Sabbath and enforced rules such as, "no TV on Sabbath (unless it's a Jesus movie)," "no eating out on Sabbath," and "no shopping on Sabbath." They knew the Bible said to keep the Sabbath, and they did their best. But for a child, doing things "because the Bible says to" isn't a very convincing argument. What I learned once I started looking around at my cousins and my classmates was simply this: keeping the Sabbath was a drag.

"Yes, God blessed the seventh day and hallowed it," my teacher continued. "That means He made it holy. He made the seventh day for us to rest and spend time with Him. He made the day for us. Wasn't that nice?"

I nodded, because I knew I was supposed to. Really, I didn't think the Sabbath was nice. I didn't think of the Sabbath as God's crowning act of Creation, or the seal of His authority. I certainly didn't see it as a gift. On the contrary, I saw it as a curse. I figured if God wanted to make a day for *my* benefit, surely He could have done a better job. What was there to like about the Sabbath? *I* didn't want to take an afternoon nap like my parents did. I wanted to *do* stuff—stuff that would get me some friends.

I wanted to get my ears pierced like so many girls in my class—but Adventists frowned on jewelry. I wanted to eat the bacon at Grandma's house that my cousins inhaled and that smelled so good—but Adventists didn't eat pork. I wanted to enter the same dance classes my classmates went to and wear the cute costumes they wore—but dance was on Saturdays, the Sabbath.

And I had never understood that line about spending time with God. How was I supposed to do that when I couldn't even see Him? It didn't make sense.

I sank lower in my seat and smoothed the pleats of my despised dress. I sighed again. Eight more hours until sundown.

All the way home, my face frowned out the window on the rolling farmland around me, a world to which I did not belong.

* * * * *

At first I thought I'd like living in the country, having my grandparents and cousins just down the road from us, scattered in a cluster of dairy farms and fields and woods in which to play. I liked my new school, with its eagle for a mascot and the spinners, slides, and monkey bars. That hour-long bus ride, because we were the first on the route, was OK because the driver played the same country radio station where Dad was a deejay. At first I liked our new house—Great-grandpa Abner's house.

We'd moved in July, and I had spent the rest of the summer before first grade breathlessly exploring the nooks and crannies of that house and digging treasures from the attic—antique paper dolls and a blue Cinderella gown among them. There was more to be found in the buildings that dotted the property: a granary, a dilapidated garage, a well house, and a barn. I found old baseball cards, paint cans, bicycle parts, bows and arrows, and more—plenty of fodder for my imagination to run wild. But with the coming of the school year, the fantasy world shattered.

Besides having my eyes opened to how "weird" my church was, something wasn't right at home. Mom was not there. Dad took me, alone, to meet Mrs. Myers at Meet-the-Teacher night, in the same building where he had attended elementary school three decades earlier.

I overheard Dad telling Mrs. Myers that night, in a low voice, "Her mother is in the Treatment Center right now." My teacher looked at me with pity and said the secret was safe with her. A few weeks later, when Mom returned, life went back to usual. And we didn't talk about her hospitalization until several years later, when it happened again.

---

1. As opposed to one of the other well-documented personality types: sanguine, choleric, or phlegmatic. You can find these personalities described in many places by many different authors (sometimes the personalities go by other names), but I love Florence Littauer's treatment of the personalities in her book *Personality Plus* (Grand Rapids, MI: Fleming H. Revell, 1983), which was recommended to me by a good teacher friend, Julie, who uses this information to "decode" her students.

Chapter 3

Elephants in Our Home

1994–1997

Lie: My family was a mistake.

*M*om's bare feet made a sucking sound as she peeled them, one after the other, off the blood-red linoleum, muffin pan in hand. That morning she wore gray cargo pants and Dad's blue flannel coat as she served breakfast.

Mom set the muffins down in front of Kyle and me—Betty Crocker blueberry, one of our favorites. "Eat quickly now, so you don't miss the bus." Dad's coffee brewed as he stacked his work papers and ad copy by the door. He still worked for the radio station, but now, instead of deejaying, he sold advertising. No matter where we sat in the kitchen, we could all feel the icy breeze slicing its way through the towels stuffed in the doorframe.

Minnesota seemed colder that winter. I was in fourth grade, and Kyle was in sixth. Mom had been home for three years. We'd been in New York Mills elementary for almost four, with the exception of a failed attempt at church school.

My parents got sick of hearing me complain that I didn't fit in at school. In second grade, also my second year in Minnesota, Mom decided we should attend church school. There was only one problem: there wasn't one nearby. So, when our church board decided to start a school, Mom volunteered to teach.

Unfortunately, it only made me hate my religion more.

The new school consisted of six kids—three from one family, none of them my age—and my mom was the teacher. Definitely not an improvement in my social life. Convinced I didn't deserve this second-class treatment, I protested all year long with temper tantrums. Every day I screamed at Mom. "I have no friends. This is stupid! I don't want to learn my times tables. When can we go back to our old school?"

The single benefit of church school was all the pianos in the building. When I could sneak away from my studies, I plunked away on the instrument. By Christmas, I had taught myself to play by ear, and my parents enrolled me in lessons. Soon after, they got me a keyboard so I could practice at home. But that didn't make up for my lack of friends.

At mid-year, the family of three moved away. We were down to Kyle and me, plus one high school student. I increased my complaints.

At the end of the year, Mom resigned and re-enrolled us in public school.

When I was in third grade, Mom tried to get the church youth group called Pathfinders off the ground. Again, our numbers were flimsy. Mom tried coaching Kyle and me through our honor books so we could earn patches for our Path-finder uniforms: learn a craft, learn archery, learn to sew, build something. But again I had no friends in the club, so I complained. I didn't want to wear the ugly brown and green uniform, or learn to march in a line, or earn silly patches. I wanted to pierce my ears, do Friday night sleepovers, and get the attention of a certain boy in Mrs. Abrahamson's class. I wanted to read Sweet Valley Twins books, play Mario Bros., and play my new keyboard. I wanted to pick rocks with my boy cousins in Grandpa and Grandma's fields so I could earn some money. I wanted to buy nicer clothes so I would look cool in front of my classmates.

Within the year, Pathfinders died too. With only a few members, it couldn't stand up to public school culture.

As I progressed through elementary school, I came to be known as a "brain," "dictionary," and "reader" by my classmates. All my teachers loved me. Some of my classmates hated me. Nonetheless, I finally made some friends. My best friend was Heidi, a distant cousin who shared our last name, was one grade ahead of me, and lived just down the road. Life could only have been better if I could have skipped a grade and changed churches and moved out of our dreary house.

* * * * *

As we munched muffins, I watched Dad and Mom dance around each other in the kitchen, much like they danced around each other's lives and the elephants in our home. Mom cooked for every meal, waiting hand and foot on Dad and Kyle and me, but Dad was always on his feet at mealtimes too. He had to have things just so. Freshly brewed coffee got thirty seconds in the microwave. Each square of the waffle was carefully filled with precisely heated strawberry topping. Slices of bread were buttered the moment they popped from the toaster. He didn't make a big deal of his habits, and he didn't expect anyone else to take them on; he just did them. Like clockwork, he ran five miles every other day. He watched football on Sundays. He played classic rock from sunup to sundown, only switching to Christian cassettes on Sabbath mornings.

Maybe he thought Mom took care of herself like this too. But she didn't. She never put herself first. She trailed behind the rest of us, handing Dad the letter he needed to mail, handing me my homework, and Kyle his permission slip. When we tumbled through the doorway in the afternoons, she had freshly baked cookies waiting for us, fresh sheets on the beds, and notes on our pillows. Some days she didn't take time to change out of her cargo pants and flannel, or to even pull her dark, wavy hair into a ponytail. But she always supplied what *we* needed.

Occasionally, she took a part-time job outside the home, but these never lasted long. She was first and foremost a homemaker.

"Mom, it's so cold out today," I grimaced, peering out the window and into the black morning. "I really don't want to walk down the driveway today. Can Dad drive us?" Our driveway was a quarter mile long.

Dad was juggling freshly sprung toast and retrieving coffee from the microwave. "I can't, Linds, I have six minutes to finish breakfast before I get late for work; I gotta keep moving here."

"I know what we'll do," Mom piped up in her can-do voice. She started toward our hand-painted cupboards, now decorated with decals. "Just give me a minute . . ." she trailed off, pulling potatoes from the sack on the counter.

"What are you doing?" I wrinkled my nose.

She stabbed at the skins with a fork. "I'll just pop these in the microwave for a minute, and you can hold one in each hand as you walk down the driveway. That should keep your hands warm!"

She was right. As Kyle and I braved the dark morning and breathtaking winds, the potatoes warmed our palms. They stayed warm almost until we got to the end of the driveway. I chucked them into the ditch and climbed into the glowing yellow bus, shivering as a wave of heat blasted my face.

Christmas arrived a few weeks later. That year, the weather was so cold we'd had to shut the living room door to conserve heat in the rest of the house. I'd moved out of my room and was sleeping in Mom and Dad's room near the remaining working gas stove. Kyle had stayed in his room, a.k.a. the walk-in pantry that had once housed my great-grandmother's canned tomatoes and jam.

Our tradition was to open presents on Christmas morning. Whoever woke first got to wake everyone else, and then we gathered under the tree in sweatpants and sweatshirts and passed around our treasures. That year, we'd had to stuff a tree into our kitchen, but it was the most beautiful tree we'd ever had—a bonus Mom had earned from her side job of making Christmas wreaths.

I didn't mind the close quarters that Christmas. We seemed closer to each other, huddled around that tree in the kitchen, opening our few gifts. That year, Mom and Dad let us each open one gift on Christmas Eve, because the evenings, so close and cramped, got so long.

I got the Minnesota author Laura Ingalls Wilder's book, *The Long Winter;* some puzzles; and a bag of M&M's. I knew my gifts were paltry compared to the gaming systems and pool tables my classmates were getting, but I didn't care. All the items, so few and so rare, brought joy. As we sat around the kitchen table putting together one of my puzzles, drinking hot chocolate, listening to Dad's mix tape of silly Christmas songs, Mom reading aloud Christmas letters from our relatives, I actually felt warm.

Who needed expensive toys when you had family?

* * * * *

Indeed, even as a melancholy, I realized I had a good life. When I thought of early childhood, I thought of camping trips, Easter egg hunts, neighborhood parades, and bedtime stories. After we moved to the country, I spent my summer days swimming at the community pool, checking out books from the library, and playing in softball leagues. My life was filled with so many good things, in fact, that I barely had time to notice the elephants that camped in our corners. For a long time, Mom and Dad did a good job of shielding Kyle and me from their troubled marriage, and the strange diagnosis that took Mom out of our lives for a time every few years. That's why I could devote so much of my melancholy to Sabbath morning protests and after-school objections.

It was not until fifth grade that I caught a glimpse of both elephants, when Mom acted funny, and Dad the next day took her to the hospital, or "the loony bin," as some of my classmates called it.

* * * * *

Before they left, Mom pulled me aside, eyes flashing with terrible import. "Linds," she whispered, "remember what I told you."

"What do you mean, Mom?"

"I'm not sure if I can come back here—oh, not because of you and Kyle—because of your dad. I can't come back if he's going to keep throwing me in the hospital like this." Her voice quavered. "I didn't want to tell you, but we've been planning to divorce for a long time."

"What?" I gasped.

She lowered her voice. "We wanted to wait until you guys graduated, but I don't know if I can do it. I'm worried for all of our safety."

When Dad pulled Mom from my arms, Mom and I were both crying. I watched as he pulled her to the car and as she snatched her arm away. "Don't touch me!" she snapped. "Help!" she screamed, casting her eyes about wildly. Her gaze caught mine.

"Mom!" I sobbed, lurching forward. Kyle hung back in the doorway.

"Stay back, Lindsey," Dad warned. "That's enough, Su!" He motioned to the car. "We can do this the easy way, or we can do it the hard way."

Mom's body went slack. Finally, she climbed into the car, because there was no one to answer her cries for help.

Later, I asked Dad if they were really going to divorce.

"Where did you get that idea?" He wrinkled his brow, paused on the seat of his chair.

"Well, she kind of made it sound like . . . like you guys were going to, um, split up . . . or something." I looked down at my feet.

Dad sighed. "You don't have to worry about that, OK? Mom is just sick right now, and she doesn't know what she's saying. We're not going to divorce. So don't worry about it. OK?"

"Hmmm," I mumbled, feeling worried.

"Your mom has something called bipolar disorder. It means she needs to take medicine, because when she doesn't, she says some crazy things. I'm sorry you had to hear that."

He paused, waiting for me to answer.

"Oh," I said dumbly.

"I know it's hard to understand," Dad tried again, "but don't worry. Mom is where she can get help now, and soon she'll be back, and things will get back to normal."

I tried to take Dad at his word and forget what Mom had said. But for some reason, I couldn't dismiss her words as easily as Dad seemed to. What if there were some truth to them? But, just like Dad said, once Mom was again medicated, she slipped back into our lives without event and without comment. Soon things got back to "normal," and we found ourselves again playing our familiar parts, which reminded me of one of our Sabbath School songs: "With Daddy in the family, happy, happy home . . . With Mommy in the family, happy, happy home . . . With brother in the family . . . With sister in the family, happy, happy home." We were good Christians in a happy family, and over the next few years, we did what good Christians do. We all got baptized.

Dad and Kyle took the plunge together in 1995, and I followed suit in 1997, at age thirteen. But I'm not sure any of us was ready.

On the night of my baptism, I still had no concept of a real relationship with God or Jesus—much less any idea how to accomplish such a thing. The one thing I knew was that when you got to be a certain age in the Adventist Church, baptism was the thing to do.

I understood that being dunked underwater symbolized being buried with Christ. I understood that I was then to rise to a new life marked by love for God and obedience to His Word. But as I paced in my too-small room in our too-small house, all I could think of was my outfit. I wasn't ready to be baptized, and I knew it. There had been no mighty inner change in me, as I thought there should be.

Nor had I noticed a big change in my family members after *their* baptisms. We still lived the same as we always did. We didn't have regular family worship times. We didn't pray together, with the exception of meal times. And we didn't read the Bible—at least not together.

After I was baptized, I felt numb as the adults in the congregation congratulated me. At the end of the night, I just wanted to peel off my sticky clothes and go home and forget about what I had done. Just like I figured, I didn't feel any different.

I wish I had taken my baptism more seriously—and my family members had done the same. Because in just one year, we were all to pass through a different set of waters that would nearly drown us. Finally, after playing the game of happy family, our elephants would suffocate us.

Chapter 4

Bombshell

Summer, Fall 1998

Lie: I can never tell.

I had big dreams the year my life crumbled. Days before I turned fourteen, my family moved into a newer, nicer house just outside of town. I thought life could only get better from here. I was starting to find my place in life, and it didn't begin and end with being the class nerd.

I had started marching band and taken a trip with the band to Michigan that summer. I had joined and excelled at volleyball. I had decided I would make varsity by my freshman year, and I would become the class valedictorian. I had gained a best friend in my grade now, Sarah. I was finally starting to enjoy lunchtime and passing periods. And I had been asked out for the first time ever by a cute boy in my class who, miracle of miracles, lived next door to our new house.

Best of all, a girl named Samantha had joined my church. Exotic, fun-loving, boy-crazy, and *Adventist,* Samantha became my new best friend. We may have looked like opposites—she had dark brown hair, a creamy Hispanic complexion, and a full figure at thirteen, while I was blonde, pale white, and flat chested—but our uniting trait was our religion. Finally, I had a friend who understood the adversities of being Adventist in public school! Unfortunately, Samantha didn't go to *my* school, and she didn't live near me. Our church was the halfway point between houses thirty miles apart. Still, seeing her once a week brightened my church life. She became my reason for *going* to church. She made me look forward to summer camp. She became a singing partner when the music leaders asked me to do special music. She was the one who had finally convinced me to get baptized with her. Yes, life was looking up.

But one August night, everything changed. It started with a car ride home from Valley Fair, Minnesota's biggest theme park, where Dad, Kyle, and I had spent the day with the church youth. Like so many times before, Mom had sat out the fun to tend to the house. This time, she was unpacking from our move.

Dad waited until we turned onto our street to break the mood. Kyle and I were still reliving the thrills of the day—that delicious lurching as the Wild Thing plunged straight toward the ground, the slight burn on our cheeks from the blazing sun—when Dad asked me a question.

"Lindsey, I need you to do me a favor. Can you ask Mom if she stopped taking her meds?"

Not again. Not now. My mind raced. I had noticed Mom's strange behavior that morning. We all had. We just hadn't said anything yet. Our trip to Valley Fair had been planned for months.

I wish the day could have stopped right there, but it didn't. We had to pull into the circular gravel driveway at 11:00 that night. We had to get out of the car, trudge up the wooden steps of the deck, walk into the entryway (which finally kept out the cold), and then pass through the kitchen with its cheery wallpaper, bird border, level linoleum floor, and oak-stained cupboards. And then I had to climb the stairs that ascended from the kitchen and confront her.

Dad and Kyle waited in my bedroom below. Actually, we all felt this was the best way. She got angry when Dad questioned her, but I could usually coax her to talk.

I found her surrounded by open cardboard boxes, sorting through high school papers and family pictures—things that should have waited until after the dishes and laundry detergent were unpacked.

I took in the scene sadly. The manic behavior was unmistakable. But at least I knew, or I thought I knew, how we could get back to normal.

I greeted Mom, and she peppered me with questions about our day. I told her I had something to talk to her about, and she suggested we pop popcorn, make hot chocolate, and make a night of walking down memory lane together. That's when I cut to the chase.

"Mom—please, don't change the subject. Did you hear me? I said I was worried about you."

Suddenly, like a runaway puppy who's been caught, she wilted. "What, Linds? What do you want to ask me?"

"Mom . . . did you stop taking your medicine?"

"Yes," she answered, surprisingly solemn, and I sighed with relief. Usually that admission only came after a fight.

"Why, Mom?" I asked, even though I was sure of what she would say: she wasn't sick.

When, quietly, calmly, simply, she said, "I'm pregnant," my heart stopped.

What? How, when I knew that Dad had been "fixed"?

In stunned silence I began to wrestle with a fact that seemed more like fiction: Mom had cheated on Dad, and now there was a baby on the way.

In those heart-stopping moments, I clung to the hope that maybe, just maybe, her mental illness was to blame. Maybe Mom wasn't in her right mind when she conceived this baby. Maybe she was too manic to realize what she was doing. Just a fluke of being unmedicated. Just a technical error. Oh, I hoped it was!

But no. Mom shattered that hope when she told me she had stopped taking her meds for the baby's health.

I retreated downstairs that night, heavy with a terrible knowledge. Dad and Kyle were waiting. I knew they expected to hear what we'd heard every time before: Mom was off her meds just because she wanted to be. For a few moments I held in my hands the power to shatter their world.

Numbly, I went into my bedroom. I closed the door. And then, with the two of them sitting on my bed, I broke the news.

Dad put his head in his hands.

Kyle kept shaking his.

Both of them asked, again and again, "Are you sure?"

My cheeks burned as the words formed bitterly in my mouth—as I relayed again and again news that was not mine to tell.

* * * * *

Two months later, the four of us sat around a table in a dimly lit room. Mom was back from the Treatment Center for the fifth time in my life, but this time she was three months pregnant. The outside air had turned cool, leaves swirled, and the sky was gray with the promise of snow. There were no windows in the counselor's office, and as my parents explained the situation to Del, a gray-bearded man in a sweater vest, I felt a vault door closing.

The horrible facts were these:

Mom had cheated on Dad.

His name was Ray. He lived fifteen miles away. And he was in rehab for alcoholism. Oh. And he, unlike our family and entire community, was black.

The baby growing in Mom's tummy was going to be black, which meant we could not pretend he was Dad's.

That night we were like a secret club, preparing to stage a major deception. Soon, Mom would be banned from leaving the house—just like we were all banned from sharing the secret beyond these walls.

"You mean you haven't told anyone, and you don't *plan* on telling anyone?" Del asked incredulously. Mom and Dad shook their heads.

Because of their religious convictions, my parents never once considered abortion, and divorce was a last resort. Instead, they wanted to make every effort to work things out, which might mean giving up the baby for adoption. And with the adoption option on the table, my parents figured, *Why involve the church or our extended family in the affair?* Anyway, winter was coming, with the suffocating snow that trapped people in their houses until spring; it wouldn't be that hard to hide Mom until she delivered. So, the plan was this:

Keep Mom at home once she's showing. No church, and no family events.

Keep all baby talk within the walls of our home.

My parents figured that by the time the baby came, we'd have a better plan in place; until then, we'd deal with our emotions by talking to Del.

"And the kids—they are not to tell their cousins, friends, or anyone at school?" Del asked.

"I don't *want* to tell anyone!" Kyle piped up, his eyes fierce.

Del waited for him to go on, but Kyle said nothing more.

"I suppose that's understandable." He sighed, then turned to me. "And what about you, Lindsey?"

I shrugged. "I don't know." I really didn't. I knew I wanted Mom's illness and her indiscretion out of the public eye, but the baby? Something about this plan seemed ridiculous. I agreed to play along . . . but still, I wondered if it was even a game we could win. I felt that, eventually, there would be no hiding the baby, and I wondered if it wasn't better to just get it out there now instead of later. What were we going to do, raise a baby through adulthood within the confines of our house, and then, one day, loose him (or her) on the world?

"The hardest thing in the world is to keep a secret," Del warned us, adding that if our family was matter-of-fact about the situation, eventually others would accept it.

But the others in my family didn't see it that way. They wanted to bury the problem because they thought that was less threatening. I wasn't so sure. Could this plan be more damaging in the long run? I tried to be glad my parents were staying together for now. Maybe they *could* make it work. Maybe we *could* get back to the way we were. I kept telling myself this, because I couldn't fathom life any other way.

Chapter 5

The Bud That Blew In[1]

Winter 1999

Lie: I have to hide.

*I*t was wintertime, and Mom was definitely showing. Mom and I went outside for the mail, shielding our eyes from the sun's glare off the snow banks. The road we crossed to get to the mailbox had iced over, and the lid was frozen shut. Mom pulled harder on the handle the second time, but it was frozen so solid that as she tugged her feet slipped. Down the ditch she tumbled, landing belly-first in the snow.

It happened so fast. Some feeling like adrenaline surged through me, but I couldn't make myself help her up. Was the baby OK? Would Mom have a miscarriage? For a moment I felt frozen, like the winter world around me.

Eventually, Mom got up. She was OK. She said she had fallen on her side, and she thought the baby would be OK. I mumbled something like, "Good," but remained silent all the way back to the house.

* * * * *

Throughout the pregnancy we stuck to our decision to not tell friends or relatives. No one in the family except me could see airing this secret in our "perfect," clean community. It was so unthinkable; so humiliating, so awkward. So, we kept the secret. Instead, Dad and Kyle became angry, yelling and swearing at inanimate objects and Mom; Mom became like a ballooning ghost, wandering around the house with a vacant look in her eyes; and I became the repository of all these secrets.

Our house became a battlefield of accusations, the release of pent-up rage and shattered dreams. Words I'd never heard at home flew back and forth through our walls. Our "family time" became synonymous with shouting matches wherein Dad and Kyle blamed Mom, and Mom protested that Dad had never given the support she needed. Dad yelled at Mom for calling Ray; Mom defended herself yet again. Kyle screamed, over and over: "Just GIVE HIM UP!"

We batted around the adoption option up until the birth. There were times we all seemed ready to reconcile; we'd decide to give up the baby, and then we breathed easier for a few days . . . until Mom waffled again and said, "No, I just don't think I can." Then, the circus started all over again: the blaming, the yelling, the tears, the swearing. Kyle especially took it hard when the tides turned, yelling things like, "All you guys ever do is go back on your word!" "Why should we want to keep it?" "We didn't ask you to go out and do that!" "I shouldn't have to deal with this!" "We were all looking forward to getting rid of the problem!" "I just want things to get back to the way they were."

For the first time in my life, I found myself without words. Suddenly, with everyone else yelling, screaming, and crying, I couldn't voice my feelings. Since I had always been the "problem child," I figured I had taken enough of my parents' attention. So, I stopped my tantrums, conceded the limelight to Kyle, and started writing, filling up journal after journal.

> *I feel like I have to grow up ten million times faster, and when I look at the world around me, my friends, cousins, whoever . . . I feel mad at others for having such happy, perfect, minor-problem lives. I feel mad at them because they can't see inside me and see all the wrenching pain that's tearing me apart, which is unfair, I suppose. But I can't help being mad at them. I'm almost surprised that all the turmoil bubbling inside me hasn't seeped to the outside and people are noticing it. I'm amazed at how easily people can be fooled.*

> *What a difference there can be between the inside and the outside of a person. I've been holding it in for six months. It sucks. Now, when I'm in public, I feel removed from the atmosphere. Like I'm just a kind of vapor, observing on the outside, like I'll never be like them again (if I ever was). I just feel different; like I've seen more of the hurt and pain of the world; like I can't find common ground with any of them anymore.*

Three days before the baby came, we were still debating whether or not to keep him—it was going to be a boy. We went to one last family counseling session and we listed the pros and cons of keeping him.

Two days before the baby came, a husband and wife couple from church visited and stayed for nearly five hours talking with Mom and Dad. They were one of the few families who knew what was going on. Before I was kicked out of the room, I heard Dad say something that terrified me: "I'm at the point where if she wants to keep the baby, she can just take him and leave."

The next night, as we sat around the living room, Mom rocking back on the recliner, Dad perched on the edge of the couch, and Kyle and I sitting cross-legged on the floor, Kyle asked Mom, with tears sliding down his cheeks, "Don't you love us enough to give him up?"

Mom didn't answer.

While Kyle and I slept that night and into the next day, Mom went into labor and Dad rushed her to the hospital. The baby was born on Dad's birthday, just like he'd predicted months earlier, upon hearing the similar due date.

I went through my daily activities as usual, including track practice after school, and then Dad took me to the hospital to meet the baby. Kyle stayed home.

"Have you called the adoption agency?" Dad asked, tight-lipped, as soon as we passed through the doorway. Tentatively, I approached the bed. My breath caught in my throat as I caught a glimpse of the brown-skinned, black-haired baby in Mom's arms.

Mom said she hadn't.

"Are you going to?" Dad crossed his arms and leaned against the doorframe.

Without looking up, Mom shook her head. She handed the baby to me, and I fumbled, afraid I'd break him. As I held him in my arms, tears pooling in my eyes, I knew Mom was right not to give him up. I wondered if, by feeling that way, I was betraying Dad.

* * * * *

The day Mom and the baby came home from the hospital, we all sat down to supper together around the table and didn't mention a word about the sleeping bundle by the doorway. Mom asked me how track and classes and band were going. Kyle just scowled. Dad looked tired. I wanted to see and hug and kiss the baby, but I was afraid to anger Dad or provoke Kyle. So I sat uneasily like the rest of them, until the baby let out a little cry.

I couldn't help myself anymore. I jumped up and raced to his side, scooping him out of his car seat. I saw then that he had been wrapped in a blanket from the hospital, because we had no clothes, no blankets, nothing here for him.

What a mean entrance into the world you've had, baby, I thought, holding him closer. *And the days ahead don't look much easier.* That night I went to bed troubled for this nameless, unwanted baby, and worried for my whole family. *What's going to happen to us?* I wondered.

* * * * *

Within a few days of the baby's entrance into our home, I thought I saw hearts softening. Every night all four of us made at least one stop by his sleeping quarters (a corner of the living room) to check on him. Even Kyle, who wouldn't look at him on the first day, was holding him and playing with him a little. Dad had started feeding and changing him, and sometimes I caught him just gazing at him. I wondered what Dad was thinking, but I was too afraid to ask. The only thing he said was, "This is Mom's plan. She wants to keep the baby around just long enough to get us all to like him."

If that was Mom's plan, I hoped it was working.

When several weeks had passed with no decision made, Mom and I decided the baby had gone nameless long enough. While Dad and Kyle played basketball outside, we sat on her bed discussing names.

"What do you think, Linds?" she asked. "I was thinking of something from the Bible. What about Joshua, or David, or Adam?"

"Hmmm. I like Caleb," I said, stroking the top of the baby's head. His hair was getting curly, and I liked to unfurl the coarse tendrils between my fingers.

"Caleb . . ." Mom repeated. "Caleb. I like that too."

I looked up, a grin starting at the corners of my mouth. "Can I start calling him Caleb, then?"

"I like it," she said. "Caleb it is."

It was then that I began to think of him as my brother.

---

1. This chapter title refers to my little brother, Caleb, and comes from a poem I wrote my junior year in creative writing class. The assignment was a metaphor poem about our family. I have reproduced it here:

Rebuilding From Ashes

My family is a house that's been raped by a fire:
My father is the framework, collapsed and smoldering.
My mother is the quilt that kept us warm, singed now forevermore.
    The baby is the flower bud that blew in with the smoke, now growing
        strong in the aftermath of ruin.
    My brother is the lawn that was scorched into blackness, but that is
        sprouting again, greener than ever.
    And I am the ashes, yet swirling in tumult, not knowing when, or where,
        to come down.

(December 2001)

Chapter 6

A House Divided

Spring 1999

Lie: I have no "home."

I huddled on my bed, wincing from the screaming outside my room. In my journal, I wrote: *Things continue to be pretty heated around here. Right now I can hear Dad yelling at Mom through my door. He's demanding answers. He said he needs some hope. I heard him say, "Give me a chance." I also heard, "I just can't do this."*

That day my parents had come to a decision—we were going to keep Caleb after all. Mom and Dad had told me the news earlier, after returning from a new counselor who must've said some magic words to Dad. While I was elated at this turn of events, I worried at how Kyle would react. I was camping out in my room while Dad and Mom broke the news.

"I'm so sick of this!" Kyle's voice projected into my room. "All you guys ever do is go back on your word."

One good thing about our new house was that I finally had a door on my bedroom. That extra bit of privacy had allowed me to secretly start an exercise routine, for which I donned only a sports bra and shorts while trying to perform the moves in Karen Amen's *The Crunch*. In hopes of attracting a boyfriend that year, I intended to flatten my abs, which, as it had come to my attention, were much too flabby. Now that I was in junior high, I had to undress in front of the other girls for gym class and volleyball practice, and I quickly noticed that I didn't match up. I couldn't do much about my comparatively small bra size, but I *could* do something about my flabby stomach. Soon, I hoped boys would notice me for more than my impressive vocabulary.

I just wish I had someone to hold me and listen to me, I scribbled in my journal, combat still firing outside my door.

One bad thing about that door was that it was far from soundproof, and it opened almost directly onto the living room, where all the "family discussions" were held.

Dad is usually so tense and on edge. He really scares me sometimes by how he talks in the clenched-teeth sort of way. He looks like he's gonna explode. He really surprised me when he said it'd be harder for him to give up Caleb than keep him. Boy, was that a different tune.

"It's over! We're keeping him. I'm not strong enough not to keep him!" he conceded now.

"No! We can't keep him!" Kyle's voice climbed to a panic. I rolled my eyes and resumed writing: *Kyle says that if Caleb stays, he'll move out. Says he can't stand living here. And, well, a lot of the time I can't either. It's a constant conflict; it seems there are never times when everyone is happy. There's always someone going through an emotional cycle, if not all of us at the same time.*

"What do you want me to do?" That was Dad's voice again. "Do you want your mom and me to get a divorce? How in the world am I supposed to please everybody? I'm just trying to provide for the family—and having a baby around hasn't made *that* any easier."

"I'm sorry for the extra cost, Daryl, but we're a package deal," Mom chirped, repeating a phrase we'd been hearing ever since Caleb got his name.

And Mom is being pretty stubborn. At least Dad has said that he doesn't want a divorce. I don't know about Mom. Last weekend she went to see Ray, and I found out that they hugged. Dad got really upset about that, but I think that's been cleared up, too. Old news.

I don't know much else. I just know that I am sick of this. I'm sick of my life.

* * * * *

The next day, Sabbath, found us back at it, only this time I was on the other side of the door. Ironically, the worst fights took place on Friday nights and Saturdays. Our "day of rest" had become our day of war.

Things weren't going well. Dad was rethinking keeping Caleb. Now, the sacrifice again seemed too great.

"If we keep Caleb, then I have to work harder, longer, and have less freedom," Dad said.

Kyle nodded his approval; with Dad on his side he could relax a bit. But this swing vote had the opposite effect on me.

"But Dad, I don't want us to split up." My voice came out high-pitched. "If Mom and Caleb are a package deal, then you can't give up Caleb without giving up Mom."

"But we can't keep him!" Kyle glared at me.

Mom remained silent.

Dad groaned. "Nothing works, because somebody ends up unhappy in each situation." He turned to Mom. "I don't suppose you have any fresh ideas?"

She took her time to answer. She looked exhausted. "Well," she finally began, almost in a whisper, "I don't want to stay where I'm not wanted. And it's clear that Kyle doesn't want me here."

No! my brain screamed. I turned to glare at Kyle. That idiot was going to ruin any hope we had!

"Mom, I want you here!" I pleaded.

She looked at me tenderly. "I know you do. Thanks, honey." She patted my leg. "But you know that if we end up moving out, you are always welcome to come live with us."

"Aghh!" I couldn't help letting out a gasp. That wasn't what I wanted! I wanted the five of us to stay together, none of this splits-ville junk. Why should that be so hard? In the back of my mind, an ugly thought reared its head. I knew one reason why it was so hard—I knew Mom wasn't over Ray.

Now, I ventured a question I had postponed asking. "Mom, if I were to go and live with you and Caleb, would you walk away from Ray for me?"

When she said, "Let me think about that for a minute," my heart sank.

"Well, I think you've already answered that question." Dad shot her an accusing look.

"Hold on just a minute, Daryl," Mom fired. "Sometimes people just need a minute to gather their thoughts."

"I would think that wasn't a hard question to answer."

"Yeah," Kyle chimed in. "How is that supposed to make us feel, Mom? It's like you don't care about me and Lindsey anymore."

I flinched at Kyle's words, because they seemed true.

"And have you thought about Caleb?" Dad added. "How can you go back to 'Chocolate Chips' and put Caleb in that atmosphere? Does Ray even have a job? He doesn't, does he? What does he do all day, anyway? Does he do *anything* productive? Is that really the kind of man you want raising your baby?"

"Daryl, that's not fair. You're making judgments and you don't know anything about him."

Dad scoffed. "I know he was in rehab for alcoholism when you met him. I know he doesn't have a driver's license." Dad's voice climbed higher with every syllable. His face turned from one shade of red to another. "I know he must be good at taking advantage of women, if he got *you* to pay him any attention. How did that schmuck do it, anyway, Su? What lies did he tell you?"

My insides curled with each accusation. I clutched two fistfuls of carpet beneath my crossed legs, hardly daring to move. *Better not say anything.* I couldn't bear to look at Dad when he was this worked up; I fixed my eyes on Mom. What would she say to get out of this one?

"I know you're angry, Daryl, but do you have to use that language in front of the kids?"

"Maybe I do, if it gets the point across!"

"Well it doesn't," Mom shot back. "It shuts down the conversation. And I won't sit here and let you badmouth me in front of my children. We'll finish this conversation later." She stood, scooped up Caleb, who had started crying, and slammed her bedroom door—the door right across from mine.

Dad stood next, muttering obscenities. I watched through lowered eyelids as he stalked off. The front closet door creaked open and a basketball bounced on the linoleum. Then the hinges of the outside door groaned, and he was gone.

He's playing basketball on the Sabbath, I thought.

I looked over at Kyle, who sat frozen, like me. But unlike me, he looked calm.

"What?" he asked, seeing my narrowed eyes. "Why are you looking at me like that?"

I stood on unsteady feet. "Don't you realize what you're doing?" I choked. But it was no use arguing. I stumbled to my bedroom, the contours of all that was familiar blurring before my eyes.

Chapter 7

Cover Blown

Summer, Fall 1999

Lie: I have to protect myself.

The last day of eighth grade came. My friends and I were ready for summer and boyfriends and freedom. Summer in Minnesota for fourteen- and fifteen-year-olds meant biking around town in packs, showing up at one another's houses unannounced, bridge-jumping, swimming in lakes, and playing summer recreational softball. For some it meant smoking and drinking and sex. My goals for the summer were these: (1) train to make varsity volleyball in the fall; (2) convince Mom not to leave; (3) continue to keep our secret as long as I could, because I didn't know any other way to live.

Now Caleb was two and a half months old, and my friends still had no idea what was going on at home. I wasn't sure, either. Mom wouldn't agree to give him up, and Dad couldn't decide to keep him. Kyle remained angry, and I remained confused.

Unlike Kyle, for the entire summer I begged Mom to stay. We were no more decided on what we would do than we'd been at the beginning, but I tried to put it out of mind. Mom and Caleb were still there, and that was what mattered. I tried to tell myself everything was OK; meanwhile, making varsity volleyball became paramount.

With the nicer weather, I started running to get in condition . . . down our gravel road, into town, past the high school, the community pool, and finally to the track, where I ran laps. I was getting lean, and I liked lean. As my feet pounded the pavement, I focused on the eagle mascot in front of the school and my goal: soon, I would wear the blue and white varsity uniform. I would play ball with the senior and junior girls. And I would make a name for myself. With these goals, I could almost forget what was going on at home. But soon forgetting would be impossible.

45

* * * * *

Mom became careless at hiding Caleb. One day my friend Danielle called, and Mom answered the phone while Caleb screamed in the same room. Later, when Mom told me to call Danielle back, I exploded. "What do you want me to say? How am I supposed to explain *the baby* she heard in the background?" I wasn't just asking for Danielle's sake; I wanted to understand too. How was I to understand that baby in the background? How was I to understand my family? More to the point, did I even *have* a family anymore? What was going to happen to us? How could we go on living like this?

I told Danielle the noises she heard were from the TV, but I knew this lie couldn't hold much longer. It was only a matter of time.

On a warm July morning a few weeks later, Danielle showed up on my doorstep, saying she needed a place to hang out while her mom ran errands. I pasted a smile on my face, but anger churned in my stomach. How bitter. Not only had I become the middleman between Mom and Dad and Kyle, but now I also had to present our situation to the world.

Smiling stupidly, I opened the door and let Danielle inside. Strewn on floors and countertops were baby toys, bottles, and blankets.

"Babysitting?" she offered, with a look that said, "I'm not stupid. Are you finally going to tell me?"

I knew the gig was up.

I gulped. "Come outside, Danielle. I want to tell you something."

After that day, the truth started trickling back to me from a few brave classmates, but only a few, who dared ask, "Do you have a black baby brother?" And I said, "Yes."

When my friend Lynn asked this question and I started crying, she assured me, "It's OK, Lindsey. Everyone has junk in their families. No one will like you any less."

I couldn't tell Lynn that was not what I was worried about. I wasn't worried that people would think less of me. I didn't even worry much about what they would think of my family. Staying together was all that mattered, but I felt it in my gut: we didn't have much longer.

* * * * *

As the autumn days turned cool and leaves began to fall, I began to detach, just like Mom. I spent my afternoons at volleyball practice, while Mom filled cardboard boxes and scouted apartments an hour away in Fergus Falls, a town we all knew because of the Treatment Center. Kyle and Dad went about their days as if our lives weren't about to change forever. As my body became lean and hard, so did my emotions. They had to, for me to deal with the pressures I now felt as the lone ninth-grade varsity volleyball player.

The volleyball players in my grade resented me, but coach had warned me this might happen. Mediocre people, lazy people, didn't like to see others succeed, coach said. They only wanted to bring them down. One teammate said I looked like I had chicken legs in my varsity spandex shorts; another tripped me one day as I was running lines. I gritted my teeth and told myself I had worked for this, they had not. In the back of my mind I wondered how they could be so mean, when they knew what was going on at home. I guessed I must have been putting up a good front for them to attack me as they did. So I looked impenetrable, did I? Then that's what I would try to be.

I clung to the coaches' praise when they said I worked harder than anyone else. The senior girls made snide remarks behind my back and said I didn't deserve varsity. I just kept running, perfecting my serve, waiting hopefully on the bench. And I joined Future Leaders of America, resumed piano lessons, and took a small part in the fall play. When Mom officially announced that she was leaving, I didn't have energy left to get angry. Volleyball supplied plenty of other people to get angry at.

After three games, I had gotten absolutely no playing time, either on varsity or the B team. The other girls snickered at my misfortune. "Serves her right!" I heard through the grapevine. If I wasn't getting playing time during regular games, there was just one option: tournaments. Tournaments didn't count toward our season record, so coach was happy to grant all players equal time. But there was a problem: tournaments were on Saturdays. Never before had I felt so conflicted about keeping the Sabbath. Volleyball was the best thing in my life right then. But how could I improve as a player unless I played in the tournaments?

This is when I started wrestling in earnest with my faith. Rather, with my religion's "rules." As far as I could see, volleyball tournaments offered me many benefits. Church, on the other hand, offered me nothing.

So I decided to play.

Kyle was the only one who went to both church and potluck the day of my first tournament. Mom hadn't been back to church since she'd started to show, and Dad left right after the service to come see me play. Our family was divided yet again, this time over the Sabbath. Which meant that now everything about volleyball—the rejection from my teammates; the lack of playing time; and finally, even the playing time, because it was on Sabbath—was laced with pain.

One day when I was complaining about my volleyball woes, Mom looked at me with a worried expression and said I was abnormally stressed out. The very next day she took me to a counselor, who diagnosed my problem with a tidy little label—depression—and prescribed a tidy little solution—Zoloft.

* * * * *

One week later, when Mom had packed almost all of her things, she sat down next to me while I was watching TV. "Talk to me!" she pleaded.

I gave her a weird look and went to play my keyboard.

She followed me. Then she sat on my bed and listened while I played.

"You play so beautifully," she said. "I'm going to miss that."

I snorted. I figured she was just saying it because she was leaving, and soon she wouldn't *have* to hear me play anymore. It wasn't true, of course. Mom was in just as much pain as I was, but I could only think about my feelings in that moment.

After a few minutes, Mom gave me the familiar line. "Lindsey, you know you can come see me anytime you want."

I ignored her and plunked out the tune to "Breaking Up Is Hard to Do."

"Won't you say something, Lambie?" she pleaded.

My mouth was hard. "There's nothing left to say, is there?"

The next day, I came home from volleyball practice to an empty house and a crockpot of chili.

"Where's Mom?" I asked Kyle. But I already knew.

He shrugged and replied, "Fergus." We didn't talk about it anymore.

Just like she'd silently passed through her months of pregnancy, she quietly slipped out of our lives.

Chapter 8

Leaving Dad

2000–2001

Lie: I can run from the pain.

Mom and I sat in her small kitchen in her new, small apartment, spooning Blizzards. I was spending most of my weekends there now, and each Saturday night was girls' night. Mom and I rented movies to watch after Caleb went to bed, or we took Caleb swimming at the YMCA, or we got a Dairy Queen treat, like tonight. I helped care for adorable little Caleb during the day, and I told Mom about my woes on Saturday night. Usually, I talked about how my teammates ostracized me, or which boy I currently liked, but that night I asked Mom, point blank, "So why did you two ever get married in the first place?"

Mom answered all my questions that night, starting from the beginning of my parents' relationship, and when I returned home on Sunday, Dad filled in even more details.

Here is the story I pieced together:

When Dad was twenty-three, feeling unsatisfied with small-town farming life, he moved to Thief River Falls, Minnesota, to attend community college, and he rented a room in a house next door to Mom. His first impression of her, as he watched from his upstairs window, was of a pretty brunette washing dishes at the kitchen sink. When she noticed him watching, Dad remembered, she quickly drew the blinds. The next time Dad spotted her, she was walking home along the manicured lawns of downtown Thief River Falls, and he offered her a ride. She accepted.

In Dad, Mom said she found the man she had never found in high school, or at home, for that matter. He said he "didn't smoke and he didn't toke," and he was the first guy she had heard even mention God or prayer. Mom's father, my grandpa Frank, had died of cancer when she was only five months old, leaving my grandma Marie, to raise six children all by herself. By the time Mom met Dad—a fun-loving farm boy and, now, college deejay who loved people and loved life—his innocent, cheerful nature was a welcome respite.

Mom and Dad dated for the two years they attended community college, and then they moved to Fargo to finish their degrees at Moorhead State University—English for Mom, social work for Dad. Near the end of their college careers, Mom proposed to Dad.

"I had a bad boyfriend in high school," Mom told me, "and I felt guilty for the stuff I'd done with him. I thought that if I settled down with your dad—this non-drinking, extroverted guy—that would reconcile my past."

"I never planned to get married," Dad told me. "I liked my life the way it was, and I didn't see a reason to change it."

Mom had to ask twice before Dad said yes.

Before the wedding, Mom and Dad both waffled. Mom said plenty of people warned her about marrying Dad, because he wasn't Catholic, and she should've listened to them. Not because of his religion—she was questioning Catholicism by that time anyway—but because there just weren't any sparks.

"We were really too young," Mom said. "He tried to break up with me a few times (I had never had that experience before), and I didn't believe him. I guess I latched onto him and wouldn't let go."

They tried to see a Catholic priest, but even he had reasons not to marry them: Dad wouldn't commit to the idea of children, and Mom wouldn't commit to raising children in the Catholic faith.

So, they turned to Dad's church, the same Lutheran church where most of his family still attended.

"And the only counseling the pastor gave," Mom said, "was this: Good, better, best. Never let it rest. Until the good becomes the better, and the better becomes the best." Mom's jaw tightened. "For the rest of the counseling session, Dad chatted with the pastor about a trip he'd taken."

"The pastor made Mom bawl at our wedding rehearsal," Dad told me when I asked him for more details. He wasn't able to tell me why, but Mom said it was partly because the pastor misrepresented the passage about wives submitting to their husbands. From their union, two and four years later Kyle and I entered the world.

* * * * *

I asked Dad once, after Mom moved out, why he didn't take time to read the Bible and pray, either for himself, or with us.

He caught the anger in my eyes and returned it. "Because I don't have time; someone needs to pay the bills. Someone has to cook the meals and provide for you kids."

"Don't you think praying and reading the Bible could help, though?" I asked, daring him to disown the religion he and Mom had forced on me. I didn't know if it could really help, but I wanted to believe it could. "How are you gonna get through this?"

He only shrugged. "Well, it hasn't done anything for me yet. I know that." After a pause, he added, "Music is the only thing that's never let me down."

Really? I wanted to scream. *Is that all you have to say for our faith after all these years? It hasn't done anything for you? Why did we even bother?*

I stormed off, not sure who I was more disappointed in, God or Dad.

Soon, I stopped going to church altogether so I could work at the city bakery on Saturdays and play volleyball. Maybe Dad and Kyle wanted to continue pretending things were OK, and maybe God was still in His heaven. But it was all a façade to me, and I didn't see any point in keeping it up anymore. Plus, I figured, if Mom and Dad didn't have to live by the Christian principles they purported to believe, why did I?

I was fifteen years old, and all I could see in my future was a never-ending soap opera. *When will it be over?* I pleaded to God. But it never ended. Not even after Mom and Caleb left. Now, the drama only shifted shapes. "That schmuck," as Dad called Ray, moved into the apartment complex where Mom lived, and I visited them at my own risk.

Dad and I grew further and further apart during my freshman and sophomore years, as I developed an attitude along with my independence. I got my ears pierced even though jewelry irked Dad. We had a major blow-up when I let my Zoloft run out and Dad went ballistic. I scribbled in my journal that night that he was treating me like one in a herd of cattle who just needed to be tranquilized. *I think I understand how Mom feels, now, when people try to force her meds on her,* I wrote.

Dad was convinced that if I didn't get that medicine in me, I was done for. "You might as well just drop out of school now," he lamented between expletives. He called Mom to chew her out: "Why aren't you making a bigger deal out of this? You better come and get her *now*—make sure she sees that psychiatrist tomorrow and gets that medicine in her!" By that time, it was spring of my sophomore year, and I was on the varsity softball team. I wondered if Dad just wanted to be able to watch me play in the next day's game.

I started to seriously consider moving in with Mom.

I sat down with Dad a few times and tried to explain why I wanted to leave. He heard me out while I gave my reasons: I missed Mom and Caleb. I had never fit in with the kids in my class anyway. And most of all, I just wanted a new start. But he maintained the same position: "You have so much going for you here. How could you possibly leave? You're about to start your junior year; you'll finally be a starter on the volleyball team, and senior year you'll be valedictorian. That's what you've always wanted, so you couldn't possibly move to Mom's." Discussion closed.

It was true. Those things were what I *had* wanted—those things, along with a boyfriend. I couldn't overlook the boyfriend factor, because it was becoming even more important to me, the longer I lived without a confidant. I had told Samantha a little about my home life, but we saw each other so infrequently that I hardly bothered trying. I was just plain lonely. I hoped I could find a place to fit in, and a good boyfriend, in a new school.

The only boyfriends I'd managed to attract in my class of sixty were ones I didn't want. After the short-lived summer romance of the boy-next-door in eighth grade, I noticed Hunter coming onto me in tenth grade. He would pull his chair over to my table at lunch and flirt and give me sideways glances. Though I really didn't like him in that way, I liked the attention he gave, and when he asked me out after we kissed for a game of truth or dare (my first kiss ever), I couldn't say no.

Four months later when he broke up with me, I suddenly forgot how I once wished he'd do exactly that. His confession, "I just stopped having feelings for you," hit me hard, especially because I suspected he had his eye on another girl.

The icing on the cake came later that week, when Mom went off her meds and back into the hospital and Caleb went to stay with his daycare lady. In the midst of all these terrible events, Dad and Kyle were nowhere to be found. They must have been out playing basketball or tennis or at an open gym night—while I wondered what I was supposed to do in the meantime.

I decided to take two hundred aspirin.

In the middle of a balmy summer night, Dad again found himself racing to the hospital for a mental illness emergency, but this time he followed the ambulance that carried his daughter.

When I got out two days later, my stomach pumped, a new counselor lined up, and a suicide prevention plan in hand, Dad was all smiles: his daughter was "better." He turned up the radio on the way home and sang along to classic rock songs, and that's when I knew I couldn't stay with him any longer.

* * * * *

I turned seventeen two weeks after the aspirin incident, and, with my savings from the bakery, I bought my first car and filled it with my things. I would take Mom up on her offer.

The night before I left, I decided to drink for the first time ever. Both an accomplice and an alcohol source were easy to find, and at the end of the evening, when I staggered into the house a little tipsy, Dad hardly looked up.

"Have fun with your friends?"

"Sure. But [yawn], I'm tired. Gonna crash. See you in the morning."

"OK, sweetie, good night," I heard as I stumbled to my room. I remember feeling cocky that it was so easy, if also a little disappointed that it was.

The next day I informed Dad I was moving out.

Standing on the threshold of that house of so many secrets, Dad didn't have much left to say, and I didn't either. Seeing my packed-up car left Dad speechless. I'm sure he hadn't really believed me. In a few weeks Kyle would be leaving, too, to go to college. For the first time in his life, Dad would be living all alone.

Spilling ripe ears of corn into my arms, Dad merely said, "Here, take some. You can take some to your mom." As my black Chevy Corsica rumbled out of the driveway, his tear-stained face filled the doorway.

Chapter 9

Life at Mom's

2002

Lie: I can find the love I need from a guy.

Now I went from our sweet country house to a smoky apartment complex where single moms worked late and little kids ran wild. These were second-string apartments, where people landed after failures and failed families. This is where Mom came, and where Ray and I eventually followed.

I dreaded the days Ray came over. He lived across the street doing nothing but (as far as I could tell) drinking beer, smoking, and watching TV. He was on welfare and didn't help support Caleb, but sometimes he would ask to borrow money from me, because he knew I always had cash on hand from waitressing. I never knew what he would say, or what he might ask of me. One awful night I had to give him a ride across town and discovered he was drunk. He started saying things like, "You're an angel, you really are. You're so sweet." Luckily, the car ride ended before anything happened. I thank God he never tried anything physical with me. Because of my involvement in volleyball, school plays, band, and my job, I was able to avoid Ray most of the time.

Mom was too preoccupied with Caleb and Ray and working full time to have much time for me. And she still felt too guilty over her affair and continuing relationship with Ray to return to church—which meant there was no pressure for me to go. Maybe this should have bothered me, just like Dad's lack of Bible reading and prayer, but instead I appreciated that Mom wasn't being a hypocrite by still attending church. As for me, the closest I came to church was the Salvation Army on Sundays, where I played piano for fifty dollars a week. I had given up on the idea that church could help me—I just went for the money now—but I couldn't give up the idea that God might still have some help to offer.

I had learned about keeping a prayer journal in tenth grade, when Samantha and I attended a prayer retreat. The leader handed out prayer journals that listed several columns: prayer request, date, date answered. The rest of the pages had a space for the date at the top, a line for "Bible text I read today," and a blank page labeled "What God said to me today." I used this tool off and on from age sixteen. It was during my junior year that I had my first good run. I read through the entire book of Genesis, seeking for God to speak to me. Most of the time I ended up summarizing my daily reading, with the occasional remark: "That's interesting. I didn't know Noah got naked and drunk in his tent! Talk about falling off the wagon. Gross!" After Genesis, I apparently failed to connect these stories to my own life, and I gave up this devotional practice until I was married.

Religion, church, and all things spiritual began to disgust me because I saw that they had not saved my family. I felt little obligation to God, and I let myself drift further and further away from Him, until all I had to say to Him was that He had failed me. Instead of turning to God, I turned my attention to guys.

* * * * *

I caught my first glimpse of Bryan in the lunchroom on my first day of junior year. He was tall with bleached blond hair and a green bandanna that beckoned like a green light. Like a white knight riding in to save the lost and confused princess (or a really cute guy being nice to the new girl), Bryan offered me a place to sit—and instantly became one of my first friends at Fergus Falls High School. Later that day, when I discovered I'd gone to the wrong lunch period, and when I again ran into Bryan at the public library, I figured God must have predestined our meeting. After all, unlike my previous class of sixty, my new class had more than three hundred students. What were the odds of me running into the same person twice in one day? Bryan encouraged me to try out for wind ensemble, the highest band in the high school, and I got in. Bryan, a tuba player, sat behind me, a trumpet player, all year long. A few weeks later, when we were cast in complementary roles in the fall play, *Go Ask Alice,* I was hooked. So this was why I had moved to Fergus Falls! God was going to make up for my heartache with a new, beautiful relationship.

Perhaps I should have questioned Bryan's friendliness when, after three months of me leaving not-so-subtle hints about my feelings, his perfect ideas of hanging out with me included organizing Mom's cupboards, proofreading his essays, or scrapbooking. I wasn't even fazed when the other good friend I was gaining in Fergus, Jess, mentioned that rumors had swirled about Bryan's sexuality some years earlier. I just ignored the signs and kept hoping one day he would realize he loved me, just like I loved him.

In February, when he asked me to the Sno-ball dance, I figured that day had come. The day of the dance was the best of my life up to that point. Unfamiliar good feelings washed over me as I prepared for our fairytale night, slipping on a periwinkle gown, curling my long hair, and slipping on milky white shoes. Yes, I was the princess, and Bryan, my handsome knight, was finally coming to take me away from my miserable reality.

That night *was* a fairytale. We slow-danced together many times, lingering in each other's arms on the last song. When it was time to say good night, we idled for an hour in his car, talking about our feelings for each other. I confessed how mine had been growing since our first meeting; he marveled out loud that his for me were new and surprising (*What?*)—but all that mattered was that they were finally there. And then he asked me the question I had been waiting to hear for so long.

"Lindsey, will you be my girlfriend?"

I stumbled, starry-eyed, through the front door and collapsed onto the couch: "Mom, he finally asked me out!" I went to bed lighter than I had in years. My world was finally looking up.

But one week later, Bryan came over with a solemn look on his face. "Let's sit down," he said, motioning toward that couch where I'd swooned just days ago.

The expression on his face was funny. I felt my stomach tighten as I sat a safe two feet from him.

"Lindsey, I have to tell you something. It's been bothering me this whole week, and it wouldn't be right for me to keep it from you."

Here it comes, a voice whispered in my ear. *Anytime something good happens, something worse waits around the corner.*

"Umm, this isn't easy."

"Go ahead," I said, "you can tell me," even though I wanted to cover my ears and run.

"Well, first let me say that I really thought I was attracted to you at the dance."

My heart stopped. *He* thought *he was attracted? Did he realize he wasn't? What's wrong with me?*

Bryan saw the alarm in my face. "Oh, please don't feel bad! It's not you! You're very nice looking." He looked down at his hands. "I just have these tendencies . . ."

I wrinkled my brow. Jess's warning flitted through my mind. "What do you mean?"

"Well, it doesn't mean that I don't . . . or I can't . . . like girls." He cleared his throat. "It's just that . . ."

"You're attracted to guys?" I whispered.

His head swung up. "Did someone tell you?"

"Jess might have mentioned something. But I didn't believe it."

Bryan exhaled. "Yeah. Well. I guess you could say it's true. But listen," he interjected. "It's not totally like it sounds." He shifted his body to face me. His eyes pleaded for understanding.

"I never had those thoughts until after my dad left, and I spent a lot of time in the basement alone with the computer. Well," he swallowed, "I stumbled on some gay porn, and I just couldn't stop looking."

I felt my breath leaving my body as he talked, like I was slowly deflating.

How can this be happening? I thought. I had never known a gay person before, not someone who admitted it, anyway. *And now, the only person I want to be with turns out to be gay!* It felt so wrong, so surreal, sitting there in a pretense of calm, as I received this news.

Bryan went on to describe how he'd been trying to deny those feelings since looking at the porn, but how they never quite went away. Meanwhile I nodded stupidly, like I understood.

Just when I thought he was about to end the conversation and our relationship forever, Bryan looked in my eyes and said, "But I don't want to be gay, Lindsey. I'm trying not to be. I had a friend who explained it to me using the word 'tendencies,' and that made all the difference. It means I'm not necessarily gay, but I just have these . . . well, tendencies to feel attracted to guys. But I don't have to act on them."

I sat frozen and confused, but with a flutter of hope in my heart.

"So, what are you going to do?" My voice lowered. "And where does that leave us?"

"Well, I'd still like to try things with you. Maybe we don't say we're 'dating,' per se, but I'm willing to take it slow to see where our relationship might go." He tilted his head, waiting for my reply.

I didn't think twice. "Yeah," I uttered, my breath slowly coming back. "I . . . I want to try it with you too. And if it's just some time you need, I'm willing to wait for you."

Unfortunately, I didn't understand the complexity of his struggles. I didn't realize that sometimes there's nothing you can do to make someone love you. I just knew I was going to try my hardest. So began an on-again, off-again relationship (and most of the time, a completely one-sided fixation) that lasted for the rest of junior year and a good part of senior year.

At first I thought we might make it. We hung out a lot, sipping coffee at the mall, listening to music in his room, piecing together a collage about our friendship, commiserating about our miserable parents. But while I made him mixed tapes of love songs and wrote heart-spilling letters, offered my ear and my editing skills, he seemed more interested in exploring his inner psyche than his relationship with me. I spent hours listening to him wonder aloud why his dad had left, whether he truly had depression, whether he should see a counselor, why he didn't have any meaningful male relationships, and what he should wear to the prom. I didn't even let it bother me much when his vintage lavender tux gained more attention than my dress. All the while, I waited and listened, hoping that after enough talking, enough analyzing, he'd realize what a great girlfriend I was—and want to marry me.

Yes, marry me. We talked about everything, even marriage. But whereas I was really serious, Bryan was only into hypothesizing. He loved exploring new ideas and "what ifs." "What if we made our prom outfits out of duct tape?" "What if we posed as the best couple ever and got everyone to vote us homecoming king and queen senior year?" "What if we got married and I was a musician and you were a writer?"

What if I had noticed the noncommittal pattern? Would I have still allowed him to break my heart?

The day I finally gave up on him came during senior year, on a band trip to the state hockey tournament, when I reached over and tried to hold Bryan's hand. Up until then, our physical contact had consisted of slow dancing at Sno-ball and the junior prom, and occasional friendly hugs. My reaching for his hand was a decided turn: a test to see if he would hold on to me.

After a moment, Bryan spoke up. "Let's analyze this." He held up our joined hands like they were a lab specimen. "I'm not sure I'm comfortable with this," he said, and proceeded to list the reasons, while my hand turned clammy in his. When he was done, I said, "Well, it seems like you've made your choice," and I released his hand and turned my face to the window. Something broke inside me. I had been rejected. For the first time I admitted to myself that he'd never had feelings for me; I'd been only a test subject for his wavering sexuality, until he finally concluded: "Nope, I prefer males."

After that day, I kept my physical distance from Bryan. I didn't call him anymore or write him letters. By the end of the year, he was telling me about the guys he was meeting online. Even then, I couldn't quite tear myself away, and still went to his house when he invited me over. "We can still be friends! We're good friends!" he insisted. I was too hurt, and too numb, to see what an insult this was.

Now it was too late to cultivate any other meaningful relationships in Fergus Falls. I had Jess, a cousin of a cousin from New York Mills—and she was a great one for hanging out and doing jigsaw puzzles, making me laugh, and trying to include me in other groups. And I also had Heather, my fun-loving pal who had shown up in a few classes and at other key moments to befriend me (I first met her when she co-starred with Bryan and me in *Go Ask Alice*). But all my other friendships during the last two years of high school had been eclipsed by Bryan. I had pursued him to the detriment of pursuing anyone else, and when the dating façade finally collapsed, I couldn't even talk to anyone about why. Again, I was guarding a secret for someone I loved who'd betrayed me.

* * * * *

"Come to college with me!" Samantha wrote from Texas, where she was in her first year at Southwestern Adventist University, returning to her southern roots and following in the footsteps of three older sisters.

After Bryan dumped me, I almost considered it. Before then, I hadn't pictured leaving Minnesota. Moving out of state for a college whose beliefs I didn't follow anymore didn't seem worth it. *It's better that I start over, anyway,* I thought. I didn't want to be reminded of my past by taking old friends into my new environment.

There were plenty of good colleges in Minnesota; I just had to pick one. I spent senior year collecting college mail, separating my prospects into file folders, and jotting lists of pros and cons for each. There was a problem, though. No college stood out. I spent hours trolling the Internet for the "right" college. I got my parents to drive me around the state to visit campuses. The one criterion I could nail down was that I wanted to go to a private college—more prestigious than a state college.

Samantha *did* convince me to visit her and Southwestern over my spring break. By myself I took a Greyhound bus to Minneapolis and from there flew to Dallas. I enjoyed my weeklong visit with my friend: I thought her college was quaint, and the people nice, and I couldn't believe how diverse the student body was. I enjoyed watching the students, especially the couples, and I wondered: Could there be someone here for me? *Nah,* I convinced myself. One-thousand miles from home was a headache. Plus, I thought the campus looked shabby. It didn't match up to all the private colleges I'd toured in Minnesota and Iowa: Carlton, Northwestern, Augustana, Gustavus Adolphus. Life was about outward performance in those days, and choosing a college based on outward appearances seemed as good a plan as any. I convinced myself that living in a beautiful place could beautify my life. On graduation day I cried for joy as I donned my cap and gown. So Fergus Falls and life with Mom had been a bust. But at college I could remake my life.

At college, I told myself, I would finally shed my baggage and become a new person. It never occurred to me that my baggage could follow me, or that all these years of heartbreak would make me easy prey for any guy who would have me.

Chapter 10

College Crash

2003

Lies: Follow your heart.

If it feels good, do it.

Death is the only answer.

The July before I left for college, Chad joined the staff at the restaurant where I waitressed. Twenty-two years old but as playful as a kid, he had a smile that would melt iron, or at least, the heart of a jilted girl. Metal poked through his eyebrow and tongue, and tattoos spotted his arms. He sported a buzz cut with a limp Mohawk of cheek-length bleached hair running from forehead to neck. Despite his rough exterior, I was intrigued.

After my breakups with Hunter and Bryan, I had concluded that no male could care for me, but Chad did. So, I barreled ahead full force . . . even after he told me he had dropped out of high school, had formerly been engaged, had two children by two different women, had done jail time, and had attempted suicide more than once. He also didn't hide the facts that he drank regularly and did drugs occasionally; but, he said, he was trying to "clean himself up."

August was fun, and confusing, and finally sad. For the better part of the month, Chad took me on storybook dates—sailing, picnicking, watching movies and cuddling—and in return, I wrote him breathless and elated poetry. By the end of the month, I was in tears that I had to leave Chad. No one had ever treated me like he had; he knew just what to say and do to make each moment intimate and special. Somewhere in the back of my mind I realized this experience wasn't so new and special to him—but I was too vulnerable and lonely to care.

"You're the best thing that's ever happened to me," I sniffled on his couch my last night in town. "How can I leave now?"

He saw his opportunity from a mile away.

"Don't leave, then. Stay tonight," he urged, pulling me to his bedroom.
I didn't resist.

* * * * *

Mom was sitting at the dining room table when I slipped through the door at
6:00 A.M. Her hair was unkempt, and she wore a thin nightgown and bathrobe.
Her eyes looked tired.

"Where were you all night?" she asked flatly.

"At Chad's," I answered, equally emotionless. I froze at the foot of the staircase,
readying for a quick escape.

"Come here for a minute."

I approached, with the sunrise beaming through the window like a spotlight.

"Did you have sex last night?"

"No," I lied, because it was the easy thing to say. Deep down, I wanted to tell
her the truth. But what I wanted to tell her wasn't just that I'd lost my virginity
the previous night. What I wanted to tell her really had nothing to do with that
night—which, frankly, had been terrible and scary and unwanted, except for the
physical closeness to somebody else. I couldn't put into words what I wanted to tell
her. I only knew it had something to do with not being able to tell her the truth
anymore.

"Are you sure you don't have anything else to tell me?"

"Yes, I'm sure," I said.

Another moment passed, her eyes searching mine—me unflinching, as if we
were playing the blinking game. I felt hardened. It just didn't matter anymore.
Even she must have realized how pointless any attempt at parenting *now* would be.

She blinked first.

"OK," she exhaled, glancing at the clock. "You better go get ready for college.
We leave in an hour."

* * * * *

So, I went to college. I went to classes. And I went through the motions. But
my heart wasn't in it. It was still with Chad, and with Bryan, and with my home
that was no more.

I remember driving into Saint Peter, Minnesota, the campus of Gustavus
Adolphus College rising into view like a new frontier. "Extraordinary people,
extraordinary place!" the college boasted. But I didn't feel like an extraordinary
person as I sat in the passenger seat of Mom's car, struggling to read the freshman
reading assignment, Tim O'Brien's *The Things They Carried*. I never finished the
book and didn't finish my first semester.

Before she said goodbye, Mom snapped a picture of me outside my dorm,

Pitts Hall, with me looking chubby and apathetic, hands stuffed into the pockets of my denim coveralls; and that's pretty much how I looked for the two and a half months I spent there.

As long as I had Chad back home, I made a go of things. I went to most of my classes, I did most of my homework, and even wrote a couple of news articles for the school paper. But the truth sat heavy on my heart. My plan to drop my baggage was backfiring; I was only gaining more.

I quickly realized my mistake in going off my Zoloft in the month before college. So I visited a campus counselor, who put me on a new antidepressant, Celexa. But nothing seemed to help. In addition to hiding from my classmates and floormates, I found myself taking four-hour naps, hardly able to wrench myself out of bed. I cried over the phone to Mom and to Dad that it wasn't going well—could I come home? But upon reflection, I wasn't even sure where I'd go.

Dad had crowded my old room with record albums, tapes, and CDs, and Mom had stripped my walls of my posters, changed the bedspread, and replaced my dresser with her things. So I didn't belong at college. I didn't belong at Dad's. And I didn't belong at Mom's. I didn't belong anywhere.

At some point in all of this, I met Rebekah and Easton, the kind and well-meaning Christians who took me under their wing. I hung out with them a few times and even laughed with them a little. But when I was alone, all the feelings, and all the negative thoughts, came back.

Life is hopeless. I'm pathetic. I have no family. I have no future.

And then Chad broke up with me and I went to the religious retreat, and I decided that the Christian ideal of "new life" was just an illusion—just smoke and mirrors, to distract people from the pain of real life. Maybe faith and religion and revivals worked for people who already had happy lives. But for me, they only killed off hope.

There's no use talking anymore, no use praying anymore, no use trying anymore, Satan whispered in my ear, as I left that church and boarded a bus back to campus. You could dress me up like a college student, a young woman full of promise and new starts, but you couldn't erase "the truth"—*life was hopeless, and so was I.*

* * * * *

On the Monday morning after the retreat, I filed the paperwork with the registrar, and I cashed in my food account in the form of granola bars and cereals that I would bring home to Mom and Caleb. I returned my library books, emailed my professors, and cleaned my room. Finally, I made sure to refill my Celexa. I calmly told the campus counselor and Megan I just wasn't ready for this right now. I let them think I was referring to college.

When I returned to Mom's, I wasn't in any rush. Now that I knew relief was imminent, my days were not unbearable. After five years of keeping up appearances,

I was tired, but for the first time in a long time, I was also peaceful. So, in the forty-eight hours between leaving campus and trying to kill myself, I relaxed. When I bought my cocktail of meds, to be combined with my prescription, I prided myself on taking care of my problems. When I sorted my belongings into neat stacks, I felt good about making things easier for Mom.

Then, I decided to celebrate. For my last night, I took myself out for dinner, dessert, and a bottomless cherry Coke at the popular teenage hangout where I'd sat with Bryan and Jess only a few months earlier. I didn't have to worry about being seen, because all my friends, high achiever types like me, were no doubt still going strong at their respective colleges. To add to my enjoyment, for the first time since entering adolescence, I didn't have to worry about calories.

That night I brought with me a handful of my journals, intending to highlight the many places where I'd listed the benefits of death. These excerpts would show my family that my decision was not irrational or whimsical—that my death was in fact the best thing for me; it was the only logical solution to the suffering that had resisted five years of antidepressants and counselors.

Several hours later, my stomach hurt from too much food and my eyes hurt from too much reading. I'd only made it to journal three of ten, but I had decided I'd marked enough evidence to make my point. I headed home to rest up for my last day on earth.

Late the next day, after Mom had left for work and dropped Caleb off at Ray's, I put on black dress pants and a white top, completing the ensemble with a fresh coat of makeup. There was still no big rush—in fact, I felt calmer the longer the day wore on, knowing it was only a small time until utter release. I only knew I had to be out of the house by 9:30, when Mom and Caleb would get home. The last thing I wanted was for Caleb to find me lying there. But I *would* leave my suicide note and my journals. Caleb couldn't read yet, so there was no risk in him finding those.

I made the bed, placed my farewell note on the pillow, and tenderly stacked my journals on the bedside table. Surveying my handiwork, I knew there was just one last thing to do. I got out my prescription, the pills, and the cough medicine. And bottle by bottle, sip by sip, I downed them all.

Now, to go die.

But first, I would stop at Chad's. He was the reason I'd dressed up.

"Hey-y-y-y!" he greeted, a little tipsy, when I knocked on his door.

I brushed past him into his warm living room and said over my shoulder, "I've overdosed on meds, and I'm going to go park somewhere and die." I plopped down on his couch. "But I came to say goodbye first."

He laughed and slammed the door. "Say *wha-a-a-at?*" He spun on his heel, grabbed a broom, and waltzed drunkenly around the room. The song "Everybody Hurts" by R.E.M. was playing in the background.

"Lighten up," Chad crooned. "Now it's time to sing along!"

How ironic, I thought. After several minutes of watching Chad sing into the end of the broomstick, making funny faces, and urging me to "sing along," I was convinced I'd made the right decision. Clearly, Chad didn't care. So I stormed out of his trailer into the chilly November night to find a deserted place, a place where people did not go during a Minnesota winter.

Snow was on the ground and lakes were frozen over, so I drove myself several miles out of town to Pebble Lake Beach, hidden from the highway by rows of trees. As I'd predicted, I arrived to an empty parking lot, where a lone streetlamp illuminated a small patch of pavement.

I parked far from that orb of light, killed the engine, and climbed into the backseat. I locked the doors. And I lay down. This was it. If the meds didn't kill me, the cold would.

Except that, within an hour, two police officers shone a light in the backseat window and rapped on my door. "Open up, or we'll break in," they threatened.

Green-faced and drowsy, I forced myself upright and unlocked the door.

A gloved hand shot out and grabbed my arm.

"What are you doing out here?" the officer demanded, blinding me with his flashlight.

Before I could muster words, I puked at his feet.

Chapter 11

Numb

March 1, 2004

Lies: I'm worthless and past the point of fixing.

I can hurt myself, as long I stay alive and don't hurt others.

I can fill the void with a guy—any guy.

I stepped out from under a naked showerhead onto bright white tile, four bare walls surrounding me. I grabbed one of the sterile hospital towels and caught my five feet, five inches of pale skin in the mirror and I stared, the way I used to do obsessively.

For four months I'd been trying to ignore the person in the mirror, pretending that if I couldn't see myself, no one else would be able to. But after all this time, here I still was. And here—*ugh*—was the un-pretty picture the world was soon to see.

A sweeping glance from head to toe confirmed the damage: the fifteen extra pounds the nurse had charted yesterday, and the splotchy acne the other nurse had ordered medication for.

I sighed.

After my suicide attempt in November, I'd spent thirteen days in a mental unit, then I returned to Mom's and resumed my work as a waitress. I'd also become a childcare provider at the YMCA. But I couldn't do it. I couldn't face life. So one January night, I'd had Mom commit me to the same place she'd gone so many times: the notorious Treatment Center. For the next forty days, I existed in a locked ward. It wasn't so bad. At least here there were no expectations. There was nothing to do except eat and sleep. Given my life's goals, it was the ideal place for me.

This morning I would be leaving, and the nurses expected me to feel overjoyed, excited, or something, but I felt nothing. This was not like going home after an operation, after an infection or a physical injury.

What the staff didn't seem to understand was that planning a suicide is mentally exhausting—and failing a suicide perhaps even more so. After fantasizing about having no more pain, after you've made the arrangements, written the letter, taken the pills, and driven out of town to lie down and die—it feels like a cruel joke when you wake up to the knocking of the police on your car windows . . . and realize you're still alive.

Now that my plans had failed, I felt lost. After battling hopelessness for so long, there was a calm that had come with knowing it would soon end. But now, without that assurance, I didn't know how to feel, or what to do, except to concentrate on the immediate steps in front of me.

* * * * *

My last morning at the Center went by in a blur. I filled out forms, signed up for Minnesota Care and food stamps, and gasped at a hospital bill I'd never be able pay. I was on my third prescription drug in the past three months, and I received a refill for the road. They took my vitals, weighed me, and wished me good luck. My fellow inmates—schizophrenics, manic-depressives, and other varieties of the mentally disturbed—gave me hugs and congratulations.

Thanks, I guess.

Shortly thereafter, my social worker, Peggy, came to get me. She would take me to my new efficiency apartment in town, a kind of halfway house for patients just out of the mental hospital. It would be the first time I'd ever lived on my own.

* * * * *

The place was a dingy three-room, barely big enough for me to stretch my body out in the living room or turn around in the kitchenette. The bathroom was hardly big enough to bend over. The bedroom had a twin bed and a window. The sheets, towels, furniture, utensils, and appliances, including a small TV with cable service, came with the place, but it all had to be washed. The floors and walls were spotted with grease and dirt, as if stained by past failures. Surprisingly, Peggy and I were able to remove most of the spots. The walls and floor began to look new again.

But I didn't count on being so lucky.

For the first time in my nineteen years, I had no goals. The only goal I could envision had been taken from me by doctors, nurses, and family members who had made me promise not to hurt myself. It was as if my slate had been wiped blank, and not in a good way. I had no close family, because I would not let them be close. I had no education, because I had blown college. I had no friends—except a few I was too ashamed to talk to. I hadn't died outside, but I had died inside.

Now it took every ounce of energy I could muster to exist "normally" in society.

With my waitressing job and my job in the YMCA's babysitting department, I was only working so I would not have to live at Mom's or Dad's. There was no career in the work. And there was no future in anything else.

Besides working, all I did was journal about how depressed I was. And sleep. When I could, I took two- or three-hour-long naps, but often I couldn't sleep. I eventually would have to give up and give in to the fact that I was in for a long, dreadful evening, just me and my thoughts.

Look what a failure I am. I will never be happy. My life is hopeless. It doesn't matter what I do to myself now, as long as I stay alive for my family.

So began my binging and purging. The idea came to me after I ate supper one night and sat thinking, *I just want the pain to go away.*

I didn't turn to drugs or alcohol—aside from my night of drinking before leaving Dad's—because avoiding these substances was one thing Dad and the Seventh-day Adventist Church had successfully drilled into me. Besides, I was too scared of long-term effects. What if I got a DUI ticket? What if I killed someone? What if I permanently injured myself? Anything short of killing myself, especially paralysis or something like it, would be devastating. What if I became an alcoholic and ended up worse off than I already was: no job, no money, all my bridges with family and friends burned, becoming more of a burden than I was now? No, I couldn't justify the risks.

What I *could* justify was overeating, because it didn't endanger my life—but it *did* numb the pain.

That night, I just started eating and kept going. Even after I was full from my microwave dinner, I opened my cupboards and ate what was there: marshmallows, chips, breakfast cereals, candy bars. After that, I planned my binges; I even looked forward to them. I would head across the street to the gas station with a list in my head of what sounded good, usually the most chocolaty, rich ice cream in the freezer.

I knew anyone who knew about my habit would ask me how I could stand to do such a thing to my body. The fact was, I didn't care about the health of my body—I only cared how it looked. As a woman, I felt that part of keeping up appearances was staying thin. My bulimia saved me from gaining weight in tandem with my depression, and it also saved me from questions. As long as my habit could distract me from my pain, I could maintain the façade—and no one had to know that my life was just a game.

* * * * *

My latest therapist was getting worried. After more than two months of her experimenting with antidepressants and maxing out my dosages, I wasn't getting better. If anything had changed, it was that I was finally starting to feel again: I was starting to feel angry.

I was angry that I hadn't chosen to be alive and yet "being," the one thing I had agreed to do for everyone else's benefit, was now completely up to me. No one could say or do anything to give me that desire.

What was more, my childcare job sparked anger at parents who put kids in the world without providing for their needs. And these parents made me angry at my own parents and their misguided marriage all over again. Finally, being angry at my parents reminded me to be angry at God for creating me. In the quiet of my apartment, I cursed God and life itself. I just wanted to be unconscious. Was that so much to ask?

After I told my therapist some of these things, as well as the fact that any more talking felt pointless, she suggested electro-convulsive shock therapy (ECT). But no matter how I longed for unconsciousness, I couldn't make peace with the idea. I feared that ECT, like alcohol or drugs, might screw me up even worse.

"I'll find other ways to cope," I said, and promptly began looking for a boyfriend.

* * * * *

Tim was even worse than Chad. Another dishwasher at the restaurant, Tim didn't even pretend to have genuine feelings for me. Unlike Chad, who had provided a romantic first date, complete with sailboat, movie, and transportation, Tim told me he was out of gas money: Could I spot him a few bucks for a movie rental and give him a ride?

For our first date, Tim got his ride *and* his movie, and I got to sit with him and his three roommates in a dirty, smoky apartment over a Laundromat watching a bloody Quentin Tarantino flick. What girl wouldn't swoon?

When he winked at me the next day in the galley and asked if he could come over to watch another movie—this time, my choice (but I still had to pay for it)—I giggled with pleasure. Within a month, he'd convinced me to not only give him rides, pay for his movie rentals, and do his dishes, but also to give him sex.

The fourth and last time I stooped to this level, we were at his apartment in the late afternoon. By this time I knew he was using me, but I hoped he would invite me to stay the night, so I wouldn't have to face the darkness alone.

But later, while we watched movies with his roommates, he stood and announced, "I'm tired; I'm going to bed." Without even looking at me, he said, "See you at work, Lindsey."

His words hit me like a punch in the gut. Less than a week before, I had mended a pair of his shorts and left Hershey's kisses in the pockets. What had I done wrong? As I sat in a daze, one of Tim's roommates said to me, "Don't take it personally. Tim is a jerk. You can stay and hang out with us if you want; we don't mind the company!"

"Thanks," I mumbled, trying to muster a smile. And for half the night I did stay, watching R-rated movies and inhaling secondhand pot smoke. I took solace in Bubba's words; he told me he'd seen Tim give a dozen girls the brush-off, and it had nothing to do with me. I vowed not to do that again. Next time I dated someone, I would make sure he wanted more than just rides, movies, and sex.

When the topic shifted to Bubba playing on the community college football team with Chad—Chad!—my heart leapt. I had pushed Chad out of my mind until now, but a familiar voice whispered to me: *Chad is the male who has cared for me the most in my life.*

"Is he still in town, do you know?" I asked Bubba in what I hoped was a casual voice.

When Bubba answered that he was, my heart leapt a second time.

I could do worse, I thought, glowering at Tim's bedroom door.

* * * * *

A few nights later I drove by Chad's trailer park, letting my car idle ever so slightly. The blinds in his window were drawn, but a light glowed from within, and there was his red Mustang out front!

So it was true! Chad was in town, and if I wanted to reconnect, I could. I started fantasizing that we could go back to the magic of the previous summer. And just thinking about that magic (never mind how it had ended) made me feel better.

I took some time to think over my options, and finally I decided to write Chad a letter. That way, if he felt like I did, he could make the next move. If he didn't, then I would have avoided an awkward conversation.

While I waited for Chad's reply, my four-month grace period at the apartments expired, and I moved into a nicer place. It was a cute, ground-level one-bedroom that looked like a gingerbread house from the outside. It sat in a U-shape among the other gingerbread apartments, a patchwork of buildings painted in light blue, salmon, and olive green colors.

The week I moved in, Tim left a message on my cell phone saying he was think-ing of me and asking if we could get together. He'd been fired from the restauran a month earlier, and I hadn't seen him since. Against my better judgment, I gave him my new address and invited him to help me unpack. He showed up with a four-pack of beer and one thing on his mind. Just minutes into the tour, he was lying on my bed and trying to pull me on top of him. But this time I was ready to fight.

"You know, your roommates were right; you don't really want a girlfriend, or a relationship, do you? Is that why you've had so many girls over to your apart-ment? Bubba was telling me . . ."

"What?" Tim spat, sitting up. "What did you say to my roommates?"

I backed away. "Hey, don't blame me for your reputation. They were just warning me about you."

Tim shot up and out of the bed.

"I don't have to take this. I'm outta here!" He stormed out of the bedroom and through the kitchen, and made it almost to the front door before turning on his heel. I watched in amusement as he flung open my Frigidaire. "I forgot my beer," he growled, before slamming the fridge door, and then the front door.

"Take it, you perv," I muttered to his retreating figure, "cuz you ain't getting anything else from this apartment tonight."

* * * * *

Saying no to Tim empowered me. I still wasn't sold on living, but I started to feel that there might be something better out there for me. My new apartment was near the community college, and I signed up for two summer classes.

Now that I was returning to college, I called up Jess and Heather, my Fergus high school friends, and we started hanging out again. My Corsica had died a few weeks back, and I found a Cavalier that I could pay for in cash. I also decided to acknowledge God again, and apologized for my previous attitude. I started praying, and I started attending church again with Mom, who had recently joined the local Adventist church.

I still was not consistently keeping the Sabbath, and I was still binging and purging, but I figured any step toward embracing life was a step in the right direction. With that mindset, I signed up for more classes in the fall, telling myself they didn't have to amount to a degree. That way there was no pressure.

* * * * *

On the first day at community college, one year after my first day at Gustavus Adolphus College, I caught Tim's gaze as he swaggered through the front doors. His eyes followed my newly slimmed figure until he tripped. I walked away smirking, feeling, for the first time in a long time, like the winner.

Later that week, my phone rang at 12:30 A.M., and I answered to hear a male voice. "Hi," is all it said.

"Who's this?" I pictured Tim on the other end.

But it was Chad! He'd gotten out of jail that day, and now he was on house arrest. That was why he hadn't responded to my letter earlier.

"It's like you read my mind." He sounded dejected. "You were right; I've been cutting myself off from people, especially the people I need most, like you."

I blushed, his voice warming me from the inside out.

He said he knew I still worked at the restaurant, but he was too shy to stop in. He apologized for calling the cops the night of my overdose.

"That was you?" I asked incredulously. *He saved my life!* I thought. Surely it was a sign.

He told me the first thing he'd done out of jail was to buy *The Passion of the*

Christ. He said he was working on his demons, hadn't drank for a month, and was looking for a church.

Glory be!

We ended the phone call promising to talk soon—me feeling equally elated and confused. I knew I should be put off by his current state—he was an unemployed criminal, a college dropout, and a dejected dad who couldn't get custody of his kids—but instead, I felt pity. For the first time since getting out of the hospital, I felt as though I wasn't the lowest scum on the planet; maybe I had something to offer someone else.

* * * * *

We talked again, and within a week, I convinced Chad to take Bible studies from Mom's pastor. *What better way to help him?* I thought, forgetting that these types of studies had never cured *my* depression.

On the night of the first Bible study, Pastor Bill showed up at Chad's apartment with a DVD about Bible prophecy in Daniel 2. As Chad fixed his eyes on the screen and Pastor Bill explained how every metal from head to toe prophesied a world kingdom that had come to pass—gold was Babylon, silver was Media-Persia, iron was Greece, and bronze was Rome—I fixed my eyes on Chad.

"That's cool!" he finally burst out, as Pastor Bill finished with the iron and clay toes—the divided kingdom of Rome.

"And one day the large stone 'cut out without human hands' will come and smash these kingdoms. That will be God's kingdom, and it will never be overthrown! That's the final kingdom in earth's history!" Pastor Bill explained with an encouraging smile. "Don't you want to be part of that kingdom?"

Chad looked over at me, a grin on his face. "This stuff is pretty awesome, huh?" To Pastor Bill he said, "Yeah, I like it. I want to learn some more!"

Pastor Bill grinned, too, and set up the next meeting; I congratulated myself on a job well done. If things kept up, Chad could be baptized within months.

Driving home that night, I sent up a prayer of thanks. "God, You really surprised me. But You knew all along that there was a reason to spare my life, didn't You?" I swallowed a lump in my throat, fighting back tears of joy. "Now I think I see, God. You don't want my life to be spent empty and miserable and alone. I always thought You didn't hear my prayers about a good husband and a stable home and all that. But I had You wrong, didn't I, God?"

* * * * *

With the promise of more Bible studies, I began praying for a very specific miracle. I bought a "promise journal" addressed to my future husband . . . and started writing in it to Chad. I was pretty sure I knew how God would answer my request. The fact that Chad couldn't even take care of himself or his two children, much less a despondent wife, somehow didn't occur to me. I just kept praying it could work. I wanted it to work so badly, I didn't even flinch when he refused to go to church with me. To make matters worse, I let him coax me into bed again. Without realizing it, I was doing exactly what Mom had done by staying with Ray all these years: she'd told me many times she stayed with him because she wanted to help "bring him up"; she wanted to convert him. But while I could see her folly, I was blind to my own. At that point, it really *was* going to take a miracle to move me out of the hole I was digging for my life.

Little did I know God had already introduced me to my miracle—and I had totally missed it.

Chapter 12

My Miracle

September 2004

Truth: " 'For I know the plans I have for you,' declares the Lᴏʀᴅ, 'plans to prosper you and not to harm you, plans to give you hope and a future.' " —Jeremiah 29:11

*T*wo months before I reconnected with Chad, Samantha had come to visit me. Shortly into our visit, her phone rang.

"I'm sorry, I have to take this," she mouthed, covering the receiver. "It's John's best friend."

John was her boyfriend back in Texas, where she was still attending college, and they were having troubles. John's friend, Buc, was apparently playing mediator.

I listened as she talked about every problem with the relationship—his treatment, his silence, his failure to call, his taking a trip without saying goodbye. At intervals, she'd answer questions: "Oh, yes, I care about him." "He just acts like I'm not even worth his time, sometimes." "Do I think he'd cheat on me? I guess I could see it happening." "Why do I stay with him? That's a good question."

When I saw her fling off her shoes and lean back in my Nintendo chair, I planted myself at my kitchen sink to do dishes. Secretly I seethed; she had come to spend time with *me*. *I* should have been the one giving boy advice. I felt only a little less annoyed at the guy on the other end of the line. This was likely the only time I'd get to see Samantha before she went back to college. And these years, it was rare for me to see her more than once a year.

Didn't this dude have any scruples about taking a best friend's precious time?

An hour and a countertop full of clean dishes later, Samantha finished the call. "I'm so sorry, Linds, but I just had to talk to somebody about all this junk going on with John. It's been such a terrible past few months with him, and Buc knows him better than anyone else."

I read the distress in her eyes and relented. "Don't worry about it. I know what it's like to have boy trouble! I told you about Tim, right?" I rolled my eyes. "And now Chad is having *his* little problems with the police." I sighed. "Maybe we'll all get lucky someday and find a man like—what was his name? Buc?" I giggled a little, thinking it was an odd name.

That's when Samantha looked at me, a funny expression starting to play on her face.

"Hey Linds . . . I think I'm getting an idea . . ."

* * * * *

When Samantha first started dropping hints about setting me up with Buc, I didn't expect anything to come of it. I certainly didn't connect this faceless man to my prayer request for a husband. To humor her, Buc introduced himself to me via e-mail. To humor him, I responded. The first call was short, because I already had plans with Heather.

This time it was me putting my hand over my phone and apologizing to a friend: "Sorry, there's this guy named Buc that I have to talk to. My friend is trying to set us up. He's from Texas!" I raised my eyebrows to show how silly I thought the proposition was.

Heather just smiled. "Go ahead and talk to him; you never know!"

I smiled back, thinking, *Yeah, right.*

"Hello?" I said.

Buc and I introduced ourselves and shared our connections with Samantha, and our Seventh-day Adventist heritage. We talked just long enough for me to note that he had a nice voice, and then I apologized, saying I was with a friend and I should probably go. I thought that was the last I'd hear from him.

Not so.

Two nights later he called again, while I was out for one of my long walks, and this time ten minutes turned into four hours.

"What do you look like?" he asked. Unbeknownst to me, he'd already seen pictures, courtesy of Samantha. "She's really pretty!" he'd told her. Of course, she'd shown him my prom pictures, and now I felt like a fraud because I never did my hair or makeup like that; I didn't just lounge around in formal gowns. I had not seen pictures of him.

"Nothing special. There's not much to tell." I mumbled, suddenly self-conscious. *This is it. If he sees my frizzy hair, flabby stomach, and too-small chest, he'll lose interest.*

"Well, tell me how tall you are. What color is your hair, and how long is it?"

I told him roughly five-five, blondish brown and past shoulder length, but I was nothing special. As if he sensed my discomfort in own skin, Buc hurried to affirm me.

"Oh, see, that's nice. My ex—maybe Samantha told you I was married before—"

I told him she had.

"Well, my ex was too short for my liking. She was five-two, and I'm six-three, and that was just too awkward. But five-five, now that's about right! Christina—that's my ex—" He made an audible gagging sound, which made me giggle.

"My ex had hair that was way too short. She had it cut up to her ears, and she looked like a boy. I never liked that about her. I think a woman should have long hair; it's more feminine."

I knew Buc was mentioning his ex only to make me feel better about myself, but it worked. The longer he talked, the more at ease I felt. I was starting to understand why Samantha enjoyed talking to him.

He said he had a bachelor's degree in accounting and was in his third year of work in the finance industry.

I told him I was making a slow recovery from depression, trying my luck at a semester of community college after having dropped out of a pricey private institution.

We discovered we were both living single and lonely in small apartments, both licking our wounds from recent life failures and looking for a new start. His failure had been Christina, his college sweetheart, whom he'd married the summer after they both graduated with their BBAs from Southwestern Adventist University, the same college where Samantha and John went.

"I should have stayed and gotten my master's degree in business, like everyone told me to, but I thought I was in love, and I wasn't thinking straight. Instead, I got married, got a new house, a new car, and then, ten months later, I got nothing but a lot of debt—a house and a car I couldn't afford."

Buc was very matter-of-fact about his failures. He gave me the facts without emotion, so I didn't read much into what he told me. Rather than dwell on how devastated he must have been after losing all the money he'd been investing since age fifteen—investing, he told me, was the first passion in life, Corvettes the second—I picked up on his resilience. Sure, he'd quit his job and moved back in with his parents for a good six months, his "own bout with depression," as he put it. But I didn't see this man as a failure, as he candidly admitted he was.

After his months in the dumps, he had picked himself up, dusted himself off, found a new job and a new place to live, and moved one hour away from his parents. Now was he soldiering on in North Fort Worth, where he had no friends or family. He faithfully went to work every day only to come home to an empty apartment, working for the weekends when he drove the hour back to his parents' home and hung out with them and his two brothers and their families.

Buc's current goal was to get back to his pre-Christina financial status, and by the simple living habits he described, I could tell he would get there. I listened, amused, as he told me about grocery shopping once a month. He had his list down to a science, and he could manage the month on $200. He was proud at having discovered how he could save money by buying frozen vegetables rather than canned. "Canned is too much for one person, so I always ended up throwing out half. Now I can just cook up as much or as little as I need."

He was also proud of having had his apartment furnished almost entirely by hand-me-downs. "I got my two leather couches from an old friend who was throwing them out," he boasted. "And my bed was an old one my parents had."

When he told me things like this, I didn't think he was weird, even though he told me his family criticized him for being "cheap." I just thought he was responsible. I wasn't used to my romantic prospects being responsible, and I liked it.

Also unlike my old flames, Buc didn't have any substance addictions—except, he told me, he had a freakish propensity for jalapeños. After my first visit to Texas, I would understand what he meant: he ate jalapeños like they were chips, probably because his father had raised his three boys on spicy foods.

Besides his jalapeño addiction, I couldn't find much else wrong with Buc, except he admitted he wasn't the cleanest of guys. My mind flashed back to the kitchen counters at Tim's and Chad's houses—stacked so high with dirty dishes that I had to use both the floor and kitchen table to sort them out—and I cringed.

"I'm not the messiest, either, though," Buc reassured me, saying that Samantha's boyfriend was much, much worse, and describing the horrors of once sharing a dorm room with him. "There are certain levels of dirty that I would never descend to. I still remember the day I asked to borrow a sweater from John and I found a nest of mice underneath it in the closet. That guy is dirty, and I would never live like that! I don't care if you have gotten along all your lives. I'm telling you now—you should never share a room with your best friend!"

Buc made me laugh. He could tell me about his ex-wife and his disappointments and have me laughing at the end of each story. I told him he was fun to listen to, that I found myself laughing more than I had in years, to which he simply said, "That's just because I'm a performer," and went on to explain the results of a personality test he'd taken. Buc had an answer for everything. Despite his recent life "failure," he was confident. But not in a cocky way, like other guys I knew. He was simply sure of who he was and what he believed. He wasn't afraid to tell it like it was.

He also wasn't daunted to hear the grim truth of my story as, little by little, I opened up. Instead of being turned off by my dark humor and brooding ways, he was intrigued.

"Do you want to talk again, maybe tomorrow?" he asked after the second four-hour phone call.

"Sure, if neither one of us dies before then," I responded through huffs and puffs of autumn air. I was walking briskly up College Street, because I could never sit still for the length of our conversations.

He thought it strange the way I ended that third call, and brought it up on our fourth. "I've never heard someone end a phone call like that. Were you trying to be funny?"

"No. Just realistic."

"Strange," he mused. After a pause, "Hey, don't take this the wrong way, because

I mean it in the best way. You know, you're not like other girls I've talked to."

"How so?" I waited for him to say I was too depressing to pursue any further.

"Well, you don't just say what you think I'll want to hear. You don't always act all silly and stuff."

"That's because I'm not a silly person."

"I know. You're really serious. Too serious, sometimes."

I started to protest that I couldn't help it, what with recent events in my life, but he interrupted. "No, I like it. I mean, I don't like that you're still struggling with depression, but I think it's fascinating how your mind works. On the one hand, I see why you would be depressed. On the other, I don't understand how you can have such a low opinion of yourself. I mean, you're beautiful, and you're obviously really smart. You've got the whole package; you just can't see it."

Somewhat pleased, but more astounded, I mumbled some kind of thanks. "But you just don't know me that well yet," I added. "You aren't getting the whole picture."

"See, there you go again. You can't even take a compliment. You just can't take good as it comes. It seems that you expect the worst, and then won't let yourself be happy. Why do suppose that is?"

I began to understand why Buc had fielded so many calls from Samantha. He was fascinated by human psychology and behavior. He was a "fixer," and it bothered him when he couldn't figure something, or someone, out. I became his next project.

Each night he gave me his full attention, without expecting any physical return—something I was not used to with males. Unlike my former love interests, Buc hung on my every word—spoken or written. No matter how much I revealed about my past, he didn't lose heart. When I shared my struggles with depression and suicide, he came back with encouraging words and Bible verses and said he wanted to help. When I confessed that the only place I'd ever shared my whole story was in my journals, he even wanted me to read those out loud to him, which I began doing on our fourth call.

Somewhere in the middle of that conversation, I noticed things quickly moving from casual acquaintance to potentially much more, and I became uneasy. Within less than a week, he'd heard about my mother's affair, my parents' divorce, Caleb, my depression, my college dropout, my suicide attempt, and even my sojourn in the mental hospital. But there was something else I hadn't told him.

"Tell me everything," he coaxed. "I want to know everything about you."

"You're not going to like it."

"Try me," he countered.

Well, I thought, *might as well lay all my cards on the table. This probably isn't going to work, anyway, so I might as well let him have the whole truth.*

I told him about Chad. How I had recently reconnected, and how he had been my first. "I was lonely, like you," I added, trying to soften the blow.

After a long pause, Buc said solemnly, "Do you still have feelings for him?"

I floundered. I pictured our phone call ending within seconds, his velvet voice fading out of my life for good, if I told the truth. And I realized that, after only four phone calls, I feared there would be no more.

But I didn't want to lie. If this man was really meant to be—and he was already a long shot—he would have to accept me, warts and all.

"Yes," I admitted. "I still have feelings for him."

To my surprise, Buc didn't slam the phone down, and he didn't yell. He merely said, "Well, then I guess I've got my work cut out for me."

Chapter 13

Choosing

October–November 2004

Truth: "But God demonstrates his own love for us in this: While we were still sinners, Christ died for us." —Romans 5:8

Sometime during those first weeks of contact, I caught a vision: was Buc the answer to my prayers about a loving husband and a stable home, even if not the answer I'd expected? Samantha said she thought so. She also said we'd be "perfect" together. But it would take more convincing on my part.

"Come to Texas!" Buc urged. "If I can get you here, that's half the battle."

He offered to pay for my plane ticket, but before we could make flight arrangements, fate—or God—intervened. I showed up at my restaurant one day to find an empty parking lot and darkened windows. Under our noses, the place had been going bankrupt, and now I was out of a job. Suddenly facing a free weekend, I decided to drive to Texas. (I had quit my job at the YMCA months before.)

By now, Buc and I had been corresponding by email and phone for a month, and I still hadn't seen a picture of him. Nonetheless, I felt so sure of his character that I printed off driving directions, hopped in my car, and drove sixteen hours through the night to meet my man of the velvet voice.

He stayed up all night on the phone to keep me awake. "I want you to get here as fast as you can!" he said. "But if you need to stop and sleep, do it. I want you to be safe, first and foremost."

I was so hopped up on caffeine, chocolate, and nerves that I couldn't have slept anyway. Somewhere in Kansas I did almost doze off and was pulled over. I nearly got ticketed for speeding, but the officer took pity on a tired innocent from Minnesota: "Just watch your speed, OK?" I had to restrain my foot and prop up my eyelids the rest of the way.

As morning broke, signs for Dallas came into view, and I revived—I was almost to Buc.

He stayed on the phone with me until I pulled into his apartment complex.

"Pull around until you see building 114. You can park in any area with the red lines, and I'll be waiting for you. I'll be the guy in black pajamas."

To me, the complex looked like something out of Beverly Hills. Large salmon-colored buildings, palm trees, a pool, and manicured lawns. The weather, bright and warm, even matched. And it was October! "Wow," I mouthed as my rusty Cavalier crawled around the complex. Knots had been forming in my stomach for the past hour. Would I suddenly feel awkward talking to a man whose life I knew intimately but whose face I'd never seen? What if he didn't like the way I looked? After driving for sixteen hours, my tussled hair and rumpled pink sweatshirt certainly couldn't hold a candle to my prom pictures.

Just as my stomach clenched again, I saw him. He'd spotted me first and was waving. I waved back. He was a black blur coming into focus as my car crawled closer. *This is it,* my mind raced. *Now, I'll see if I was a total idiot for taking this trip, or if this man is really worth it.* It hit me for the first time that maybe I'd made a mistake! "What have I done?" I moaned, all the while smiling and waving as I pulled into an empty space.

I climbed out of the car, stiff from sitting, and took a few steps in his direction. Suddenly, he was there, engulfing me in a hug.

He smells nice, I thought, *and he's bony.*

"I'm so glad you made it!" he said.

"Mm-hmm," I mumbled, my face crushed to his chest.

When I pulled away, I found myself looking up into hazel eyes, sandy blond hair, and an Adam's apple that looked like it would poke my eye out. I felt startled. He seemed almost too skinny to be the owner of that full, smooth voice I'd come to love. For a moment I worried I was in the wrong place. Then he smiled—a warm, big smile that stretched from ear to ear.

"Hi!" he said, pulling back and extending his hand. "I'm Buc."

"Hi," I followed. "I'm Lindsey."

"It's nice to meet you!" His eyes were appreciative of what they saw.

"You too," I repeated.

So this is Buc, I thought, surprised at how shy seeing him made me. He didn't look like I expected. But his voice was the same. I realized I hadn't had any preconceived picture of him. To me, he'd been just a distant voice—almost like a dream that I expected to wake up from one cold morning. As of this moment, Buc was a real person, and he was present with *me.*

I felt a shiver run down my spine.

The newness of it all was uncomfortable; but at the same time, looking into the kind face before me, I knew I was in a safe place.

"Do you have a place where I can crash?" I asked, yawning.

* * * * *

I woke to see his face hovering over mine.

I hope I didn't drool, I thought.

"Hi, honey," he said.

"Hi," I replied shyly.

"I hope you're going to enjoy your trip."

"Well, it's so new. But I think I will. Can you just give me a little time?"

"All the time you need, babe," he said tenderly, brushing a wisp of hair off my forehead.

Within an hour of talking with him, his voice reassuring me again that, yes, this was the same man I'd come to know over the phone, I inched closer. How could I not feel comfortable looking in his eyes? There was no judgment, no repulsion, no hesitation; and despite his eagerness to hold me, there was no pressure. Although I'd never been privy to such a look, it was unmistakable: he was a man in love.

* * * * *

The weekend was too short. After I rested up, we had a wonderful time camped out on the floor of his apartment, talking, watching movies, even listening to a sermon on Sabbath. We went grocery shopping, and I made him grilled cheese sandwiches and soup during NFL Sunday. There was nothing fancy about our time together, but there didn't need to be. Because together felt comfortable. It felt natural.

A highlight of the trip came when Buc called Samantha. "Hey, Sam, someone came to visit me; I think you might want to speak to her."

She squealed when she heard my voice. "Linds! Is that you? What are you doing there? What's going on? Is there something you haven't told me?"

We laughed. It was true, we hadn't told her we'd been talking for the past month; she was absolutely clueless.

The other clueless party was Buc's family, whom I first "met" when Buc finally checked his messages late on Sunday.

"Oh wow! I can't believe this!" he chortled. "Actually," he added after a pause, "I can."

"What? What is it? Is everything OK?"

"Yes, yes, it's fine. Just . . . well, you'll see. Here, listen." He handed me the phone. "Lindsey, meet my mom."

What proceeded was a string of no fewer than ten messages from Margie Gendke, progressing from, "Hey, where are you? You're late to church," to "Where are you, son? Is something wrong?" to "Marcus Ray Gendke, you better be dead in a ditch somewhere or have a darn good excuse for putting your mother through this. It's been twenty-four hours and we haven't heard from you. What's going on? Call me as soon as you get this!"

My eyes widened. *Was this woman for real?* What kind of parent called her twenty-four-year-old child every single day—and left ten messages when he didn't answer?

"One with the umbilical cord still attached," Buc told me, matter-of-factly. "But it gets even better," he winked. "Keep listening."

I next heard a male voice. "Buc, dude, would you call Mom already? She's been bugging me all day asking me where you are. Call her, *please,* so I can get some peace!"

I giggled. "Your brother?"

"That's Brady, the oldest one. Keep listening!"

Again I lifted the phone to my ear.

"Hey, Buc, what's your problem? All I've heard all day is, 'Where's your brother? Can you imagine a son treating his mother like that? I didn't know I raised such a rude son. Call me if you find out anything!' Dude, give the woman a call!"

"That must be Bo?"

"Brother number two," Buc confirmed. "He's the middle one."

"Wow."

"I know. The thing is, this is totally in character for Mom."

"Wow." I repeated. I tried to imagine one of *my* parents being that involved. We did well to talk once a week. More often, several weeks passed without any contact. "What about your dad? Is he that way too?"

"Not quite. Dad is from a much quieter family, so he shows love differently. For example, he likes to give really unique gifts. He gives the kids two-dollar bills, and he gives us boys knives, because he likes to collect them himself."

"That's neat. So how often does *he* call you?"

"Actually, I call Dad every day at lunch; he's got rheumatoid arthritis and can't move around very well. He's stuck in the house a lot and gets bored."

"That's sweet, hon." I marveled again at Buc's thoughtfulness, and his thoughtful family.

"So, when are you planning to tell your parents about me? Wouldn't it bother your mom not to know you were spending a weekend with a girl?"

"Eh," he shrugged. "It would, but it's not like I deliberately didn't tell her. I've just been talking to you so much lately, I haven't taken the time."

I laughed at the contrast between Margie's and Buc's personalities.

When we kissed goodbye, a new thought struck me: *What if Margie were my mother-in-law?* I wasn't sure whether I'd like that. Buc and I had broached the topic of marriage, but I figured it would be a long time before anything ever came of it—*if,* and it was a big if, anything came of it. For now, just planning another visit was enough. Before I left, Buc bought a two-way plane ticket, vowing we'd see each other again in three weeks. I said I couldn't wait, and I meant every word.

* * * * *

But when I arrived home, something Buc dubbed the rubber-band effect hit. Even though Buc and I had confessed no less than love on our visit, I began to wonder, *Is Buc really the one I want?*

Seeing Chad again made me doubt. *I love him too,* I thought (much like a dog returning to its vomit). Out of respect for Buc, I hadn't been physical with Chad for several weeks, but I did continue to see him and line up Bible studies. Throughout, I was honest with Chad: "I've been talking to a guy from Texas," I told him, to which he scoffed, "Oh really? What's ol' Southern boy like? Got some cowboy boots and a gun?"

I told Buc I wasn't sure about us; I half retracted my confessions of love.

"Really?" he was incredulous. "But I was there. I heard you say it! You said you loved me, and it felt 'like home' being with me. You said those exact words!"

"I know, and I'm sorry. I really felt that way when I said those things. Look, I didn't say I don't want to see you anymore; I just need time. I'm confused."

He groaned. "I don't understand you. How can you say something and act the way you did? How could we have such a great weekend together and then you go back to that loser and be confused? What does he have going for him? Does he even work?"

Each great love has *some* complication. So began ours. Throughout the month of October, while I wavered, Buc soldiered on. But the longer I dallied, the angrier he became. "I don't know why I'm sticking around just to play second fiddle," he said. "Why is it even a choice?" That's when he gave me the ultimatum:

"Either choose him, or choose me. The guy's a schmuck—isn't that obvious? But if you can't see it, I can't compete with a guy living down the road; and I won't wait around for you to figure out what a mess you're making of your life. So you need to choose, and you need to choose fast."

These words fell on me with a sickening thud.

I'm not ready! My brain screamed. *Too fast! This decision is too fast!* I had known Buc for less than two months, and he was asking me to make a choice that would affect the rest of my life.

All his reasons made sense, logically speaking. But I wasn't used to making decisions based on logic. I was used to following my sinful, feeble heart. And right then, that heart was confused.

After six weeks of getting to know Buc through marathon phone calls, I thought we might, one day, have a future together. But at the moment, I *already* thought I saw a future with Chad.

Chad had waltzed into my life when I felt rejected and forlorn—he was the first person to really *want* me when I needed to be wanted so badly. After feeling dead, he had made me feel alive (no matter that he did some illegal things and, by now, had three kids by three different women). Besides, he needed me to help him clean up. I was a Christian—at least, I was trying to be—and he needed a revival.

"But you are too implicated to deliver the message," Buc groaned, when I tried this argument. "*You* are not the right one to save him, especially if he thinks he can get lucky with you just by taking some Bible studies."

I cringed. Buc spoke truth, but truth was not what I wanted to hear. I wanted to explore my budding relationship with Buc but keep Chad on the sidelines too, in case it didn't work out.

"I need some time," I said. "I'll call you when I've made my decision."

"Choose," he demanded, and hung up the phone.

After three sleepless and tearful nights, I did. I called Buc and told him he was "the one," but I wasn't happy.

"I prayed for a sign today," he merely said. "If you didn't call by tonight, I was going to end it with you. God must want us to be together."

His words were touching, but they still didn't make it easy to write Chad and tell him "I'm sorry, but Buc is my better prospect, and I'm moving to Texas to be with him." My school semester was ending soon, and with me out of money and out of a job, Buc and I had decided I should move in December.

Buc told me just to mail the letter, but I told him Chad had my Steven Curtis Chapman CD. I didn't tell Buc that I really wanted to say goodbye to Chad. That saying goodbye to him was my attempt to break from my past.

As I pulled into the trailer park, memories flooded over me. There he was, same as always: stocky and tattooed, pierced and grungy, but with a smile that could melt the crunchy snow underfoot. I remembered the first day I'd met him, when he sauntered into the restaurant and asked for an interview. Then, he was happy, bubbly, on top of the world. At that time, he was starting life over, getting a new job and enrolling in college for the first time. That was the summer before I started college too. The summer I was looking for a new start.

And now, I was moving on with my life, and Chad was still here. I felt almost guilty that my life had been redeemed and his had not.

"Hey you," he called as I climbed out of my car.

"Hi." I squinted up at him.

"Whoa, looks like you've been getting ready for some sun." He pointed to my reddened skin. I had, indeed, for the first time in my life, gone tanning, worried that if I didn't, I'd burn in Texas.

"And I see your hair is holding its color." I was referring to his bleached blond head, which I'd helped dye.

He returned my CD, and gave me a hug; and told me to check my oil before I left for Texas. Then I drove off, never to see him again, until seven years later when I'd Google him and find his mugshot for domestic violence.

* * * * *

After that day in late October, I felt my life rushing to December and my new start in Texas. And I, feeling excited about my future for the first time since before college, was ready to go.

One week before Christmas, a few days before my move, I spent a last weekend at Dad's house. Kyle was home visiting too. That's when I told him I was moving, probably to get married. He hadn't been in my life much since we'd both lived at Dad's, and he hadn't heard much about Buc.

"Don't you think you're being a little rash?" Kyle asked, wide-eyed, as we sat among Dad's music collection in my old bedroom. "Have you really thought this through? Did you seek counsel on this? Have you read what the Spirit of Prophecy says on choosing a mate?"

In the three years we'd been living apart, Kyle had dedicated his life to God and his life's work to the Seventh-day Adventist Church. After earning an associate's degree at Bemidji State University, he'd moved to California to attend the Amazing Facts College of Evangelism (AFCOE). Now he traveled the country helping with Revelation Seminars and other evangelistic efforts. His role as a Bible worker was to pique and nurture people's interest in the seminars by knocking on doors and offering Bible studies, or following up with interested persons already identified by the local church. For the first time in my life, I looked up to Kyle. I actually wanted his advice—on God, not on guys.

When Kyle told me I was being too rash, that I was making a mistake, I didn't want to hear it. Just like I didn't want to hear what he'd had to say after my suicide attempt. In the past year, one of the few talks I'd had with him was a phone conversation from the mental ward. "Why didn't you call me first, Linds?" Kyle cried. I suppose I didn't call him first for the same reason I didn't ask his opinion on marriage.

Kyle might have understood how to give a Bible study to an interested audience, but he didn't understand how to give advice to his depressed and unconverted sister. He didn't understand that what I most needed was not doctrine but a soothing voice, a nonjudgmental ear, and a hug. In other words, just what I'd found in Buc.

Dad didn't try to stop me as Kyle did. I'm not sure why. But after about age seventeen, Dad didn't try to force me to do anything. He seemed to accept my choices as beyond his control. Maybe while his marriage crumbled, he figured his heretofore straight-laced, straight-A daughter could handle herself. Now, after my lowest point, maybe he actually understood what I needed better than Kyle did. I'd told Dad bits and pieces about Buc on a series of lunch dates when he came to Fergus to sell advertising. Dad actually seemed excited to see my face light up when I discussed my groom-to-be. He said he felt relieved knowing Buc was a responsible young man in finance, because he knew his daughter would be taken care of. Perhaps Dad was just glad to see his sullen-for-so-long girl finally perk up to something, anything, and that was reason enough to let her set sail.

* * * * *

While hindsight tells me I was not emotionally equipped to be in a serious relationship at that time, a relationship was exactly what God ordered for me. Not a therapist-to-patient, friend-to-friend, or parent-to-child relationship; I'd tried these avenues, and they had failed. I had tried medication, I had tried running off to college, and I had tried a silly retreat, confusing God's power with the shallowness of some of His followers. But none of these things could fix me. Only God could do that. And He had a specific plan—one that would reconnect me with the deepest desire of my heart. I couldn't articulate it then, but I wanted a family again. After years of estrangement from my childhood family, I just wanted someone familiar, reliable, and stable. I wanted a home that was whole and healthy.

Buried deeper still was the desire to be whole again as an individual. I wanted to remember who I was and who God had made me to be, and I wanted to be able to show my face without embarrassment. Now that I think of it, what I wanted seems a whole lot like what Mom was trying to regain at the same time.

The last piece of advice Mom gave me before I drove out of her life was this: "If you get married, make sure you take yourself with you. Don't leave your past behind or try to forget where you came from. Don't leave parts of yourself out just to blend in better with his family and his surroundings. Make sure *you* are whole yourself, because if both people don't do that, you cannot be happy—and you can't be healthy."

Mom was trying to warn me that day: *Don't let yourself be silenced; don't let your past be concealed; and don't let yourself be treated as less than you are.* But some mistakes, we can't learn from others. This was one I'd just have to learn for myself.

Part 2—New Beginnings

I suppose people can have a conversion experience during a time of great uncertainty. But I have a hunch that it won't happen too early in life—not on the first few big upheavals. Looking back, I like to think it took me years of having small miracles, or even some Band-Aids placed, before I was really ready to trust God. For a long time I wanted to trust Him, but not until I saw Him sustaining me for a while did I actually learn.

My next big breakthrough came after God granted me another critical building block for my identity: the profession of teaching. Though the first year was hard, at the high school I gained my own community, one that neither my husband, nor my church, nor new friends had provided, but one that I, by my choice of degree and career path, had found. This was the first circle in Texas that I'd truly broken into by myself. The first place I went without being led by someone else. This was perhaps the first thing I could really claim as my own in Texas—my identity as a teacher. This must have been something God knew I needed before He would take me through my next big breakthrough. Breakthroughs are painful. But God knew I could handle it now.

—from my "Writing to My Roots" notebooks, October 2012

Chapter 14

One New Family, Coming Up!

December 2004

Truth: "God sets the lonely in families." — Psalm 68:6

I arrived at Buc's apartment just two days before Christmas, and on Christmas Eve morning, we rode to Houston with Buc's brother, Bo, Bo's wife, Deborah, and their two daughters, Madilyn and Megan.

Grandma's house was our destination. Every year at his grandma's, Buc's parents and his nine aunts and uncles and their families filled the house with loud voices, Diet Coke, alcohol, cards, and lots of food. They were Italians, and on the four-hour ride in Bo and Deborah's van, Bo, Deb, and Buc warned me of the chaos I would see.

"The house will be completely full."

"It's so loud you almost can't talk to anyone."

"You should see Margie and her four sisters in the kitchen—they're like hens in a henhouse. They all have to help with the food."

"And you'll recognize the sisters by their hair. All of them do their hair big and teased and blonde like Margie—it's their signature."

"And there's tons of food. If you ever wonder why Mom [Margie] cooks so much food, it's because she grew up with nine brothers and sisters. They just don't know how to make a small meal."

"Then there are the gifts. The gifts take a long time, because all the kids get gifts from every aunt and uncle. Remember how the whole living room used to be filled with presents stacked up to the height of the tree, and filling half of the room?"

"This was because of Grandpa. He passed away years ago, but if there was one thing he did big, it was Christmas. The kids didn't get much during the year, but when Christmas came, he'd saved up all year long, and he spent his whole bonus just on the kids. He always wanted the kids to remember Christmas."

Bo, Deb, and Buc were right: it was a zoo on Christmas Day, a Saturday. I sat silently on the couch taking in the spectacle. It was just as they'd described—lots of beer and Diet Coke, big hair, and big laughs—a huge contrast to the quiet Christmases I remembered before my family split up. I felt out of place the entire weekend.

* * * * *

On Sunday, Buc's family got together at Mike and Margie's for a smaller-scale family Christmas, and I accompanied Margie to the grocery store for some last-minute items. It was the first time I'd ever been alone with her.

As we were leaving the store, Margie paused, grocery bags in hand, and looked straight at me. "Buc has not been happy for a long time," she confided. "I want you to know that I was so glad a few weeks ago when I saw Buc at church. He was the happiest I'd seen him since before his divorce. And I'll never forget what he said when I asked him what was new."

She leaned in, her eyes twinkling. "He told me, 'I've got a girl on my arm and money in my pocket.' "

When she said that, I remembered that Buc was still recovering from debts his ex-wife had left him to pay off. How he was trying to get back to his premarital financial status. And how he'd said that purchasing a '69 Corvette—his dream car—would signal that "he was back," because that was what he'd had money saved up for right before his wedding.

As Margie described it, on the day Christina left, Margie had been on her way to the home of her oldest son, Brady, which was right down the street from Buc and Christina's. Brady told her, "See that moving van down the street?"

Yes, she had seen it, but hadn't thought anything of it.

"Christina is leaving Buc," Brady said.

At hearing Margie retell the story, my stomach dropped with two grave realizations. One, Buc had been hurt. Badly. And, two, I held the key, or so Margie made it seem, to either make him happy again or to crush him yet again. I headed back to Margie's house with a lump in my throat. What had I gotten myself into? I started wondering if I was well enough, or mentally stable enough, to compass this responsibility.

* * * * *

Several weeks later, when I was again sitting surrounded by Buc's family at Mike and Margie's (they got together often), Brady turned to look at me, the strange new woman in Buc's life. This was the first time I'd ever really talked to him, minus a brief introduction on Christmas. "So, tell us about yourself," he said. "Who is Lindsey?"

I froze, and so did everyone else. Everyone turned to look at me: Brady and Joanna, Bo and Deborah, and Mike and Margie. To them it must have seemed like a simple question; but to me, it was anything but.

Who was I?

This was a question I'd been asking myself ever since the hoopla of Christmas had died down. I wasn't prepared for the sadness that descended once I was left in the quiet of Buc's apartment day after day while he worked. Once again, I had no friends, no career, no plans to fill the gaping emptiness of life. It was terrifying, reliving the same displacement I had felt immediately after my suicide attempt. Again, everything I knew was gone. Again, I didn't know where I fit. Who was I? I wanted to deny the truth. Maybe I'd denied the truth during our heady months of long-distance dating. The fact that Buc was so far away had allowed me to pretend my location—Minnesota—was the problem. If I just moved, all would be well. But here I was, away from home, again. And here the truth was, still.

Who was I? Brady wanted to know.

I was a girl who still fantasized about suicide when an opportunity presented itself, like when Buc had explained how to load his AK-47. Buc thought he was just giving me a random tutorial. He didn't know that a light bulb clicked on in my head when he proudly took out his gun—and he didn't know how, for so many months before I met him, I had fantasized about finding a gun, holding it in my hands, and putting it to my head. He didn't know my detailed questions on the loading of the gun were not spurred by small talk but driven by the memory of desperation. He didn't know I was filing the knowledge away to use one day in case my emotions climbed back to those desperate measures.

"What do you want to know?"

"Well," Brady shrugged. "What do you like to do in your spare time? What are your goals?"

Frantically I searched myself, trying to think what it was I enjoyed doing these days, and what it was I wanted out of life.

"Ummm, in my spare time, I guess I like playing the piano . . . writing . . . exercising," I lied.

Those *had* been my hobbies once. He didn't have to know I didn't enjoy them anymore. He didn't have to know that those things, if I even did them anymore, were futile attempts to quell the agitation that attacked me from sunup to sundown. That they were things I now did only because I couldn't sit still for the constant anxiety pulsing through my veins.

Most days I woke between four and five in the morning, too agitated to sleep, so I would get up and run. I exercised to the point of exhaustion, because exercise was the only thing that stilled my nerves. When at Buc's apartment, I used his gym membership and spent hours of each day on the elliptical machines there. If I stayed in the apartment Samantha had lined up for me near her university, I took long walks around town. And in the rest of my spare time, I watched what I ate, now terrified of undoing my progress. I ate mostly oatmeal and salads, because I'd heard of an old classmate of mine, allegedly anorexic, losing a lot of weight on this diet. Lately, I had taken up coffee in earnest too, because it suppressed my appetite. By far the worst way I was keeping my weight in check—and the most enjoyable—was still the bulimia. That was the truth. But it wasn't an acceptable answer.

What were my goals? I gulped.

I had exactly one: to attach my nothingness to Buc. The only reason I had moved to Texas was to get married, and until I did, I couldn't set down roots or make a home. How else could I? I had no money, no family, and precious little motivation. The one thing I had in Texas besides Buc was a new job at Taco Bell. Ugh. If we didn't get married soon, I didn't know what I would do.

I decided not to even say I wanted to marry Buc. We had only known each other for four months. That answer would cry "desperate."

"My goal right now is to not work at Taco Bell," I joked.

Everyone laughed. They looked at me for a few more seconds, then, seeing my helpless shrug, Brady took me off the hook. "So you don't say much. That reminds me of when Joanna first joined the family. Do you remember her first Christmas?" He now addressed everyone.

"Yeah, yeah," the voices started. Laughter began.

Brady turned to face me again. "We were all down in Houston at Grandma's, and these Christmases are just crazy, as you know. Anyway, the house is full of Italians, some of them dead drunk, and everyone is yelling over the top of everyone else. Meanwhile, Joanna is just sitting on the couch stunned, not saying anything. So then my uncle—he's drunk at this point too—turns to Joanna and in a voice so loud he makes everyone stop, blurts out, 'Do you *talk*?' "

Everyone was laughing at the memory, and soon the attention shifted away from me to family stories, such as the time Margie, a "scaredy cat," had run out of the house in fright after someone had knocked, and she'd wasted all the bullets in the gun just trying to load it. I also heard about the time Mike and Margie were awakened by a frightening sound in the middle of the night, and Mike, in the dark, struggled to pull on Margie's too-tight jeans to run outside. Then there was the time Aunt Sharon washed an Alka-Seltzer down with a Pepsi and almost choked to death. The stories went on.

I wished I had something interesting to share. What must they think of me? I was sure I was nothing more than boring to this colorful bunch. All of them but Joanna— she hadn't changed much since her first quiet Christmas—all of them had loud voices and used them, continually interjecting, interrupting, or shouting over the other voices when they couldn't be heard. How different this was from *my* family's get-togethers.

I was relieved when Madilyn and Megan asked me to come and color with them. I quickly stood to follow.

Deb raised her eyebrows. "You sure are nice, Lindsey. They never get that attention when we're all together."

I shrugged. How could I say no? At least with the girls, I didn't have to sound intelligent or interesting; I just had to be interested in *them*. That was the great thing about kids—they were unpretentious. Megan was so unpretentious that she actually took my hand and said, before we left the room, "We like you better than Christina."

"Shut your mouth!" Deb barked. The rest of us hid giggles. I was glad to know I had passed the test with two more Gendkes.

Chapter 15

I Always Cry at Weddings

March 1, 2005

Truth: "I delight greatly in the Lord; my soul rejoices in my God.
For he has clothed me with garments of salvation and arrayed me
in a robe of his righteousness, as a bridegroom adorns his head
like a priest, and as a bride adorns herself with her jewels."
—Isaiah 61:10

In the Gendke family, there is no such thing as a missed birthday, a missed anniversary, or even a missed Sabbath phone call. After Buc and I were married, I couldn't believe that every Saturday morning without fail, whether the sun was up or not, Margie called to say, "Happy Sabbath, praise the Lord, Shabbat Shalom, I love you!" Similarly, I would get used to Thanksgiving calls at 5:00 A.M., proclaiming "Gobble, gobble, gobble!" And we knew we could always expect Buc's birthday call at exactly 10:53 A.M., the minute of his birth in 1980. No matter whose birthday it was, whether child or adult, the Gendkes gathered to honor the day. Even holidays like the Fourth of July, Labor Day, and Memorial Day merited a barbecue, so when it came time for a wedding, there was no way I was getting out of a celebration. I just didn't know it.

At first I planned a Justice of the Peace wedding (meaning, I didn't plan at all). It didn't matter to me if I had a dress, or witnesses, or decorations, or a cake. As far as I was concerned, the facts that I was alive and getting married were much greater accomplishments than any ceremony would be. It was only when Deborah insisted the family should be there that we moved the location to Mike and Margie's. Mike was a retired pastor, after all, and he could marry us as easily as anyone else.

Almost as soon as Buc and I decided on a date, I informed my parents: "We're not planning anything, really. Just a quick, simple ceremony. You can come if you want to, I suppose, but there won't be much to see."

When I told them this, it was what I believed.

"You can get back to me," I added. "And if I don't hear from you, I'll assume you're not coming." I thought I was being kind, making it easy on them to say no and save their airfare. It was an unspoken rule we'd lived by since leaving each other: Don't guilt each other; be careful with each other's feelings. Don't put too much pressure on anyone, or make a family member feel too burdened. We heeded these unspoken rules sometimes to the point that we didn't talk at all.

No longer did we yell at or accuse one another, or even bring up the bad memories, if we could avoid them. We'd outgrown that. But neither did we playfully joke around or tease one another, like my fiancé's family so easily did. No longer did we confide in one another or seek help or advice for the big issues of life. Since our last years together had been spent mostly yelling or accusing, and the years after that in cold silence or small talk, it seems we just didn't know what to say to one another anymore.

Kyle was the first one to call me back and say, "Sorry, Linds, I don't think I'll make it."

I don't care, I told myself. *He doesn't believe in this marriage anyway.*

Mom was the next to RSVP.

"I've been thinking, Linds. Even though I know you said there wouldn't be much to see . . . even though it's not a traditional wedding, I'd like to be there. I want to see my little girl get married. Would that be OK?"

I was surprised. Though a lot of mothers would have no scruples about elbowing their way into their child's wedding, welcome or not, Mom still had issues with inserting herself into her children's lives. I knew she blamed herself for our family's breakup, just like Dad and Kyle did in the beginning; ever since, she'd been tentative when it came to telling us what to do; tentative about being in our lives. She always asked permission first, as if it might not be OK.

"Of course you can come, Mom," I said, and I realized I was glad she was coming.

Dad never did get back to me. A straight shooter who took words at face value, he believed me when I told him we weren't planning anything; it didn't matter if he came or not. And I believed that myself . . . until we pulled up to the "Gendke Love Chapel," and Buc opened the door.

I stepped inside and stopped. What was previously a living room had been transformed into a beautifully adorned wedding chapel. Gauze and tulle frosted the entry table, along with lavender rose petals and, staring straight at me, a framed wedding announcement, complete with Buc's and my picture, inviting some unspecified audience to attend this day's events.

My eyes traveled farther into the living room, where the fireplace was a fireplace no more: now it was an altar, consecrated for the sacred exchange of wedding vows. Like the entryway table, it was draped in tulle, sprinkled with rose petals, and displayed an arch of purple candles. On either side of the fireplace stood hip-length white columns overflowing with baby's breath; to the side of the altar sat a white-tablecloth-ed bench with a unity candle. Everywhere I looked, I saw frilly tablecloths, rose petals, purple candles, and white and purple flowers. When Deborah had mentioned "decorating a little," I had no idea what she was capable of. As I quickly learned, Deb is an amateur wedding planner who gets hired several times a year by friends, relatives, and church members, to work magic on their special day. But all I'd known of her before that day was that she, along with my best and only friend in the state, Samantha, had encouraged me to buy a wedding dress when I'd said I'd rather not. Mike and Margie had chipped in the money, so one week earlier, I'd reluctantly tagged along with Deb and Sam to Fort Worth in search of a wedding dress. Now it was waiting for me in Buc's old bedroom—it would perfectly complement the churchy look of the living room—but suddenly, I couldn't go in.

I turned on my heel, pushed past Mom and six-year-old Caleb, and hurried back to Buc's hunter green Saturn. There, beneath the relentless southern sun, surrounded by crunchy yellow grass and the flat plains of North Texas, I sobbed.

Mom followed me and peeped her head in the passenger window. "Are you OK, honey?"

But I couldn't lift my head. I couldn't summon words. Instead, I struggled just to breathe. My tears continued for thirty minutes in the car while Mom held me, and I gasped and gulped, unable to think beyond the lies again playing in my head.

I don't deserve this. I'm not made for this kind of family. I don't know how to be in this environment.

"Honey," Mom purred in a tone more appropriate for a scraped knee.

A couple times Buc popped his head out the front door, but I waved him away. I didn't want him to see me like this. I didn't want to ruin *his* wedding day too.

When my crying subsided a bit, I flipped down the visor above me and looked at my red and swollen face.

"I can't go in like this," I moaned.

"Linds, if you're not ready to do this . . ." Mom started.

I shook my head. I couldn't call off the wedding. To do so would be to put myself out on the doorstep of the man, and the state, that was to be my salvation.

As if on cue, when I looked up again, there was my saving grace—tall, lanky, clean-cut, and bespectacled, striding to the car to save me, yet again.

Buc pulled me from his car into a soft embrace, which made my stomach tingle just as it had that first weekend. "You ready for this?" he asked.

"Yes," I lied, and we went inside.

* * * * *

Afterwards, our day went off beautifully. With the Gendkes in charge, no detail went undone. My three nieces, Madilyn, Megan, and Taylor, were given the jobs of Bible and flower girls. Bo and Brady stationed themselves in opposing corners, Brady to record the ceremony on camcorder, and Bo to snap pictures. Deb was the wedding coordinator and last-minute detail-fixer, and Joanna helped the girls get ready. Mike, of course, officiated, and Margie lined up a reception at Olive Garden. Someone even ordered a wedding cake with our picture on it and bought nonalcoholic wine so we could take the traditional cake-swapping, wine-toasting shots.

The only helper I brought was Samantha, who did my hair and makeup.

After the ceremony, Brady and Bo took turns snapping photos, enlisting Samantha's help for whole-group shots. My family pictures were quick: a shot with Mom and Caleb, a shot with Samantha. The groom's took considerably more time: Buc and his folks, me and his folks, Buc and his brothers, both of us with the family, Buc and I with the kids. That day, the Gendke men were in fine form. All had worn suits and their "black-and-white" shoes, a male Gendke tradition, and they posed like models, hands akimbo and right feet thrust out in a semi-circle.

* * * * *

Neither Kyle nor Dad called that day.

When one week had passed, I figured I really should give Dad a buzz.

As soon as he said Hello, I knew something was wrong.

"Dad, what's going on? Are you OK?" I heard sniffles on the other line.

"I didn't come to your wedding," he said. "Everyone at church is asking me why I didn't come to your wedding."

My stomach lurched.

I started crying then, too, because I knew I'd messed up. Maybe we all had. On my wedding day, I had known something wasn't right, but I couldn't articulate what it was. Now, as I cried with my father, I dimly began to understand what it was: We didn't have enough good memories, my family and I. Dad should have been there. Kyle should have been there. And I, too, should have been present in the planning of this day. We all should have celebrated my wedding.

Chapter 16

Missing Person

2005–2006

Truth: "And the Holy Spirit helps us in our weakness. For example, we don't know what God wants us to pray for. But the Holy Spirit prays for us with groanings that cannot be expressed in words."
—Romans 8:26, NLT

Three months after we married, Buc and I decided it was time for me to enroll in school again. It seemed important to my recovery that I return to college and finish what I had started. What didn't seem important was what I'd study, as I was still new at giving life another try. The thought of committing myself to an entire career still terrified me, even though a career path should have been obvious: writing was what I loved, and what I had always loved.

But I couldn't recognize myself as a writer. All I could see was a failure who needed a new start. Instead of seeing writing as a potentially professional activity, I saw it as something that had to remain personal—because it represented pain and hurt and darkness, or the part of me I could not show. To let that out would not represent progress.

Because we lived an hour from Southwestern Adventist University, I enrolled in the distance learning program and began taking generals. But after four months and fifteen credits, a major still wasn't any clearer to me—and that's why I finally went to campus and took a personality test.

* * * * *

I sat in the Career Services center, face reddening, as Steve, the counselor, read out loud the results of my personality test. "Ms. Gendke suffers from insecurity, low self-worth, and self-doubt. Because of these traits, Ms. Gendke's efforts, and the use of her talents, will be mediocre at best."

Steve stopped, lowered the paper from which he'd been reading, and peered over the rims of his glasses. "So, Lindsey, is there something you need to talk about today, besides your college schedule?"

My face reddened. I busied myself with the hem of my blouse. "I—I don't really know what to say. I guess all that stuff you just read is true."

Steve waited, saying nothing. After a moment, to break the silence, I continued.

"Sometimes I feel pangs of longing to be really good at things, like writing, or music. But most of the time I just feel apathy about my career . . ." my voice dropped, "and life."

Unlike my first foray into college, I had not entered university this time expecting to find my life's fulfillment. In fact, after ten months in my new marriage and in this new state, I doubted life fulfillment was possible anymore.

By now my numbness had turned into indifference. I wrote in my journal that I was "figuring out life to some extent," and that life at the time was just about staying busy; I could "go through the motions" to get through the day. I wrote that I viewed the world as a game to be played, a series of maneuvers to be made, until I reached the finish line. I was proud of finally being a "functioning" adult.

I also thought I was pretty clever for tricking myself out of my suicidal tendencies.

"Do you ever think about hurting yourself?" Steve's tone had dropped.

"Well, sure," I said, "but I'm not planning to *harm* myself." I paused, considering that my periodic binging and purging wasn't exactly healthy for me. Yet, it still helped me cope. Buc worked nights at this time, and I missed him when he was gone. At dusk, when he left, was usually when I binged and purged.

Steve's steel gaze prompted me.

"Umm, I used to be pretty suicidal. I even attempted it a couple times, and I spent time in a mental hospital for it."

"How long ago was that?"

"About two years ago, I guess. That was after I dropped out of college—the first time I went to college, I mean."

"I see." Steve crossed his legs and clasped his hands around his knee. "So you've been living an hour away from here, and Buc's family is here, and you said you have a friend here—Samantha, right?"

I nodded.

"OK. Well, that's good." Pause. He thought for a while more. "But up until now, you've been away from your family, and Buc's family, and your church, and you don't see Samantha much, right? Don't you ever feel lonely?"

You have no idea. Tears burned behind my eye sockets.

We didn't figure out my class schedule that day, but hearing myself talk out loud, I did figure out one thing: I didn't *have* my own life. Indeed, I had achieved my goal of attaching my nothingness to Buc.

* * * * *

At Buc's church, besides becoming "Pastor Gendke's daughter-in-law" and "Buc's wife," I was starting to be known as "the piano player." Again. As happens in small churches, it didn't take long for someone to find out that I played and recruit me. I started out in the Cradle Roll class with the babies and toddlers, playing songs that brought back vague memories from my own childhood. Before long, I was asked to perform special music, and soon I was a regular player in the worship service. These roles were the most familiar I'd yet found in Texas.

I really didn't know these people, or know much about them, except what I could glean from the gossip at Mike and Margie's on Sabbath afternoons. Every weekend we drove the hour-long ride to the "Gendke Love Chapel" and stayed *all* weekend, because our church was there and we had nothing to do at our own apartment. For most of our first year of marriage, I sat in silence on Mike and Margie's couch on Friday nights, on Saturday afternoons, and on Sunday mornings, listening to the family banter back and forth—always feeling guilty for imposing, for eating their food, for sleeping in their guest bed, and for contributing nothing in return.

We didn't socialize much with other church members because our distance made it impractical. The one exception was the engaged couple, Julie and Jarrett, who were willing to drive an hour to come see us. We went to one church campout together, and after that, we became fast friends. Julie and Jarrett were energetic and fun, and they lifted my spirits every time we hung out. I wished we could live closer to them. Both students at Southwestern, they planned to move into married student housing just as soon as Julie graduated and they married. They started lobbying for us to move into married student housing with them. I prayed we could, so that I could gain more friends at school and church.

I never had a wedding shower at the church, much less a wedding, or even a reception. Quietly, in a detached sort of way, the church embraced us. A few months after our wedding, someone took up a collection for us in lieu of a wedding shower, and we received an envelope filled with two hundred dollars. I never found out who organized the collection.

Later I would get a job at the Nutrition Center owned by Bernard, one of the church's elders, and his sons. Bernard's wife, Nancy, told me, as we were stocking shelves one day, "We were so glad to see Buc find a nice girl like you. His ex— *ooh,*" she wrinkled her nose. "We're just glad to have you. And I am personally so glad you play the piano. You know, I used to be the one who had to play in Cradle Roll and in church sometimes. That always stressed me out so much. And you do a much better job."

Other church members, customers at the Nutrition Center, spouted similar praises when I rang up their veggie bacon and supplements.

"You do such a great job with our church newsletter; we are so lucky to have you."

"You play such beautiful music."

"We're so glad you don't, you know, 'decorate.' " The elderly couple who said this wrinkled their noses and pointed at their earlobes, indicating my absence of jewelry. They didn't know I'd removed my earrings just months ago.

Meanwhile, as I became a favorite among the music leaders and the elderly, other young adults, the children of the members who loved me so much, were leaving the church. Many had already left before I arrived. "The parents were too strict. Drove their children right out of the church," the Gendkes told me on Sabbath afternoons.

After a while, I felt like the poster girl for young adults at our church. This was funny to me. I was the girl from public school and a broken family who had tried to commit suicide, and I was "more Christian" than the kids who had been home-schooled or educated at one of the many Adventist schools in the area. Growing up, they'd had the advantages of Adventist peers, booming Adventist youth groups, and multiple Adventist churches to choose from, all within a forty-mile radius. Many of these "kids" belonged to families that were entirely Adventist, and to parents who had never divorced. I started to think that faith wasn't a matter of having had perfect Adventist parents or an Adventist school or Adventist peers. It wasn't at all to do with who you had around you; it had to do with how you related to God. Most of the youth I saw were not tight with God. This wasn't only my problem. But somehow, I gave off the impression that it *wasn't* a problem for me.

But they don't know what I'm really like, I would sit thinking in the pew. They didn't know about my depressive thoughts, my bulimic binges, my nagging at Buc, or my sinful past. I wondered how this information would change their treatment of me. Would I suddenly fall from "good girl" to "damaged goods"? Would the compliments stop, and the gossip start? I figured it was best to stay silent and let them believe I was as "good" as I appeared. But it was a heavy load to bear.

One Sabbath as I sat in the back pew next to Mike and Margie and Buc, dutifully facing the front and ostensibly listening to the sermon, I felt the urge to cry. Just that morning I'd received another batch of compliments, first in the entryway from the greeters; then from Ms. Jean, the Cradle Roll leader; and finally from several other adults as I'd walked into the sanctuary. *They don't know me at all. All they care about is that I look neat and tidy and obedient on the outside, and that I can provide a service to them. I don't fit in here, I don't feel like anyone cares about me, and they're all oblivious. And when I leave today and go to Mike and Margie's, it'll be the same thing. I'll sit there looking "good," and no one will know that I'm actually very bad.*

Like so many other Sabbaths at church, I realized the sermon was almost done and I had no idea what it was about. My mind wandered its worst during sermon time. I never *tried* to tune out the message; it just happened. Later, at Mike and

Margie's when everyone would discuss the sermon, I'd chastise myself once again for being unable to join the conversation.

Nonetheless, I actually wanted to go to my in-laws' that day, just so I could escape this stifling church. "Can we go? Please?" I whispered to Buc, tugging at his trousers. He saw my red-rimmed eyes and nodded.

Back at his parents' house, we waited for the others. By the time Margie arrived, I had dragged myself outside to lie on the side of the pool, hoping sunshine would lift my mood. I didn't want to even look at anyone. I wished we had an apartment close by to which I could escape.

I heard Buc talking to Margie in a low voice, but I wasn't sure what they were saying.

When I went in a few minutes later, Margie sat down next to me and looked me in the eye.

"Lindsey, I know you don't feel good. Is there anything I can do?"

I felt my features harden. "Thank you. I don't think so. It will pass eventually."

"Well, you know you can always talk to God about it. Tell Him what you're going through. He's there to listen."

"OK. Thank you. I'll try to remember that." I just wanted the conversation to be over.

She waited another moment, and then said, "Well, let me know if I can do anything."

I doubt it, I thought. Out loud, I thanked her.

* * * * *

The next day, my malaise lingered. On the hour-long car ride back to our apartment, it intensified. I dropped my duffle bag as soon as I crossed the threshold and made a beeline for our bedroom, where I collapsed into tears.

A moment later, Buc was there, holding me, rocking me in his arms.

"Honey, what is it?"

I was gasping so hard I couldn't speak. How could I explain the emptiness, the sense of loss, to him? Every time we visited Mike and Margie's, and even at church, it hurt. It hurt seeing Buc so comfortable with his family, and all of them so comfortable with their faith. They were sure of where they came from and what they believed. No matter what happened on the outside, they could always "come home" to a predictable setting. No matter what, there would be Mike in the morning, studying his Bible at the dinner table; there would be Margie, hailing the Sabbath with phone calls and hosting big Sabbath lunches. These were memories I did not have, comforts I did not know.

I wanted to appreciate the blessings I *did* have: a wonderful husband and a steady marriage. But every time I sat in the "Gendke Love Chapel" or in church, I felt alone. I felt as though I had lost my training wheels too soon, like I had been forced out into the world before I was ready. And now there was no going back, no matter how much I longed to.

"I need some tissues," I spluttered, trying not to drip on Buc.

"What's wrong?" he tried again, handing me the tissues.

I filled several tissues, tears still flowing, and shook my head. "I can't . . . I don't . . . I just can't say." I convulsed into more sobs.

"*Shhh*, it's OK." Buc cradled my head to his chest and rocked me. "Let's pray," he said.

"Dear Jesus, I just want to pray for my wife, Lindsey. Lord, You know she's struggling here in Texas. She feels depressed about her family, and she's sad. [Buc was convinced pretty much all my problems stemmed from my family.] I hate to see her like this, and I pray You will give her some comfort. I pray that she knows what a blessing she is to me. I am so grateful to have her. Thank You for giving her to me, and help me to be a good husband to her."

Buc wasn't one to pray out loud much, but he started doing this for me when I cried. These were the only times he initiated prayer outside of mealtimes. I usually felt a little better after he did, although I didn't know if it was because of God's help or my husband's strong arms. Buc was my "rock," as I penned once in a poem. I thought he was so much stronger than me.

Years later, I asked Buc, "What do you struggle with? You seem so solid in your faith. Like when you ask God for signs. And when you take it on faith that it is God who answers your prayers when those signs come."

I should insert here that we *did* end up moving to campus to live in married student housing with Julie and Jarrett, *after* Buc asked to see a red cardinal one morning, and we did.

"You've never left the church," I continued, "even though so many of your peers did. And you know your Bible better than anyone I know, except maybe your dad."

He shrugged. "I only know my Bible so well because my parents drilled it into me. I know the prophecy stuff from helping with tons of Revelation Seminars as a kid. And I've never walked away from my faith because it makes too much sense to me—God has to be real, because all those prophecies in the Bible have come true. It sure makes more sense than evolution." He paused. "What do I struggle with? I don't have a great prayer life. I don't really know how to pray. For example, the Bible says that if you ask anything in God's name, He'll do it. But I've asked a lot of things in God's name, and He doesn't do them. What about all those good people who get sick and petition God, and He doesn't heal them? That's when I don't understand how prayer is supposed to work."

Buc told Margie the same thing shortly afterwards. "I don't have a good prayer life, and I don't know how to get one."

Margie's response to Buc? "You just need to pray about that, son."

Chapter 17

My So-Called Prayer Life

2006–2007

Truth: "And we all, who with unveiled faces contemplate the Lord's glory, are being transformed into his image with ever-increasing glory, which comes from the Lord, who is the Spirit."

"So we fix our eyes not on what is seen, but on what is unseen, since what is seen is temporary, but what is unseen is eternal."
—2 Corinthians 3:18; 4:18

I started to notice that Seventh-day Adventists in general might have trouble with prayer. I'd rarely doubted the validity of our beliefs, supported as they are with Scripture. And we are good at asking prayer for outward things, such as jobs, physical health, and other people's needs. But when it came to praying about wounds *inside us,* I didn't see a helpful or viable model.

When I was a little girl, prayer was giving thanks before meals and again at bedtime. At bedtime, I also made requests. The one request I remember making, as I peered at the top of Dad's bowed head, was that he wouldn't go bald too quickly. "Let him keep his hair, Lord," I prayed. At the time Mom and Dad stopped tucking us in was probably when that part of my prayer life stopped.

At both my Minnesota and Texas churches, we had something called praise and prayer request time. The elder on duty steps down from the platform with a roving mic and tells the congregation it's time for praises and prayer requests. Those who have something to say line up in front and tell the congregation what's on their hearts. Common praises include things like protection from an auto accident, a new job, getting over a sickness, or passing a major test. The most common prayer requests—and on any given week, these far outweigh the praises—are for physical health challenges.

After several years of these requests taking up his sermon time, my Texas pastor suggested doing away with the verbal requests and substituting a prayer box.

The church board, however, shut him down: "No, this has always been tradition in our church, and people would be upset if it went away."

So the pastor did the next best thing: he started reminding the congregation every week to keep the requests short, and please, don't mention last names! He also urged members: "Come to Wednesday night prayer meeting! That's the place to lay out your specific requests and get prayer."

I went a few times, but I didn't like the format. Just like at church, our prayer time consisted of people raising hand after hand to spill the beans on their sister's or brother's, mother's or father's, cousin's or neighbor's health troubles. Then we broke into pairs to kneel and pray about said requests. For the last half hour, the pastor stood up and "led" a Bible study; but to me it seemed like he was preaching another sermon. Just as in church, I could never keep my mind from wandering. We sat in rows facing the front. There was no eye contact, little conversation, and no getting to know one another, unless you stayed after to chat.

In all my years of church going, I had learned that prayer was this: a list of requests you make to God. It's good to throw some praise in there, too, so you might start with, "Thank You, Lord, for Your many blessings," but then you launch into a list of requests ten times as long as the praises. I learned that prayers sounded pathetic: "Lord, please be with me." There was no confidence that He was already there. "Lord, be with this and that and the other thing, or him or her or the other person." "Lord, help me with this." "Please forgive me for that." Our prayers in church were whiny, needy prayers.

My own prayers were almost all pleas for help and forgiveness: "I'm sorry that I act like You are not enough to satisfy me, God. Can You please help me not to overeat and then throw up?" They were requests for everyone I could think of. They were a forced list of thank-Yous: "Thank You that I finally have a stable place to live and work. Thank You that I have a husband who loves me and pays the bills. Thank You that I have a job even if I don't like it. Thank You for helping me not to do anything drastic to myself."

After I prayed such prayers, any relief I felt was for having fulfilled some vague requirement: I could check "prayer" off my to-do list. Beyond that, I didn't notice much extra peace. *I wish someone could teach me to pray,* I thought, but I didn't know who to ask.

* * * * *

Kyle first visited Texas ten months after Buc and I married, during our last weekend in North Fort Worth. With Julie and Jarrett's urging, and with our "cardinal sign," we were moving to campus. Buc would commute every day to work, while I attended classes on campus and worked at the Nutrition Center.

Kyle was living and working five hours away at a small Adventist boarding school in Arkansas, where he'd been hired to be the assistant dean and to help plant a church.

The Friday night he finally made it, I felt surprised to see him actually standing in our doorway. The last time we'd been together was at Dad's, the weekend before I had moved.

"Hello," he said with a grin, and I mirrored him, unable to stop grinning.

I stepped in for a hug. He was like a brick wall, rigid and unmoving, but for a stray hand that patted my back.

We parted awkwardly, and then he bent down to untie his shoes.

"You don't have to take off your shoes, Kyle."

"I know." He looked up. "It's just habit with me now. The boys in the dorm aren't allowed to wear their shoes past the entryway, so I've had to get used to it too."

As he hunched over his task, I noticed that he looked thinner, leaner than when I'd last seen him.

"Dad said you're eating a vegan diet now, is that right?" I did a mental check of my chili simmering on the stove: no meat—check; no dairy—check.

"Well, yeah," he said, straightening. "That's all they serve in the cafeteria."

"Come in, sit down. And how do you like that?"

We plopped on Buc's hand-me-down leather couches, arranged in an L, one of us on each.

"Oh, it's not the best food I've ever tasted, but you get used to it."

We laughed.

"So do you consider yourself a vegan now?"

"I guess you could call me that. I stopped eating meat before I took this job; about a year and a half ago, when I was at AFCOE. After that, cutting out dairy and stuff wasn't too hard. What about you?"

We were just moments into our reunion and already I felt inferior to my big brother. Ever since he'd gone off to Bible college, I'd gotten these feelings whenever we talked.

"Well, I went vegetarian four months after we married."

"That's good," he nodded.

"But I'm not vegan," I apologized. "It's not so easy when you don't have someone cooking vegan for you. I wouldn't even know what to do, even if I had the extra time to cook like that. Now that I'm working and going back to school . . ."

"Linds, don't worry about it!" he interrupted. "It doesn't offend me if you're not a vegan." He laughed a little. I relaxed.

"So where's your hubby?"

As if on cue, Buc walked into the room, hair still damp from his shower.

"Hey! So big brother is finally here!"

Kyle rose and extended his hand, but Buc waved it away. He pulled Kyle into a bear hug. "We can't just shake hands, man. Brothers gotta hug!"

I let out a giggle. I remembered a similar line from *Tommy Boy,* in the scene where a fat Chris Farley envelops a fit Rob Lowe. The physical comparison didn't quite work in this case: Buc and Kyle were both skinny, although Buc had by now put on thirty pounds from my cooking.

There was Kyle, dressed neatly in a short-sleeved collared shirt and khakis, not a hair out of place and rigid as a metal pole, and Buc, a few inches taller, with tousled wet hair, white undershirt, and gray sweatpants.

What will Kyle think of him? I'd wondered and worried all day long. I felt nervous for Kyle. *This must be really awkward for him.* It was the same awkwardness I faced every Friday night when we arrived at Margie's house and she hugged me, and every Sunday morning when we left . . . and she hugged me. By now I had come to expect frequent hugs in her family, but I still wasn't used to it. Hugging Kyle tonight was better than I'd done on Buc's and my first visit to Minnesota, when I'd introduced Buc to my grandpa with a handshake.

"I can't believe you shook your grandpa's hand!" he exploded at me later. I just shrugged. What did he expect from a girl who didn't remember hugs at Christmas, or anytime, with these family members?

That was the visit when Buc couldn't stop repeating something he'd been repeating ever since: "Your family is weird."

"Likewise," I told him, and started repeating it every weekend thereafter at Margie's.

"Hey, are you guys hungry?" I said to break the awkwardness. "I have chili on the stove."

* * * * *

Over supper I was happy to let the new brothers-in-law do most of the talking.

"So, how do you like your job?" Kyle asked Buc.

Buc shrugged. "Another day, another dollar. You know."

It never ceased to amaze me how apathetic Buc was, or gave the impression that he was, about his job. He was a great worker, but that would have been impossible for Kyle to know. I had already learned that the less we talked about work, the happier Buc was.

Kyle and I were different from Buc in that way. Unlike Buc, who couldn't wait to get home at the end of the day and couldn't wait to get to his parents' house on Friday afternoons, Kyle and I got so absorbed in our work and school that we let family phone calls slide. We could shut out the rest of the world for months at a time before looking up and realizing we hadn't talked to one another for that long.

Such was not the case for Buc, and so far this was the biggest contention in our marriage. He was always telling me to relax, and I was always telling him to get up and do something.

"How about you?" Buc turned the tables on Kyle. "How's the life of a dean treating you? You keeping those juvenile delinquents in line? Had to beat anyone up lately?"

Kyle laughed. He wasn't used to Buc's personality yet—this was the loud Italian personality that came out in a crowd, not the personality I'd come to know over the phone—and I always worried that newbies would take his sarcasm seriously.

Kyle handled it fine, though. I reminded myself that for more than a year he'd been knocking on strangers' doors and offering Bible studies. Surely he'd had to develop some good people skills to do such work. And a good sense of humor. It wasn't uncommon to hear of Bible workers having doors slammed in their faces or being charged by dogs.

"It's going well. The school is really a model for education. The founders, Chester and Harriet Clark, really prayed about setting up this school, and they designed it to follow counsel."

Kyle went on to describe the ins and outs of the little academy in Arkansas. It was buried away in nature, so they raised their own crops and literally lived off the land. The students only attended classes for half the day, which allowed them to learn a vocation the rest of the time. Some learned agriculture, some carpentry, others cooking or office administration. It was a self-supporting school, so this arrangement benefited both administrators and students. In fact, as Kyle admitted, it didn't pay much, but he wasn't complaining. The work was meaningful, and that was what mattered. Since Kyle's conversion, everything was about meaning, purpose, and mission. Just like his school. They were perfect for one another.

At the mention of a six-hundred-dollar stipend per month, Buc cringed. "And you can't even eat cheese," he pointed out—but something awakened in me. Watching Kyle's face light up as he told about his new mission, I realized: *I want to be that passionate about something again, too.*

* * * * *

Later that night, when Buc left Kyle and me alone to catch up, Kyle asked, "What about Bible work, Linds? You could do what I did."

I snorted. "It sounds great, Kyle," and it kind of did. After trying so hard to measure up, it sounded like a relief to do something I knew God definitely approved of. "But I can't just up and move now that I'm married."

Kyle paused, mulling over my words. "Well, maybe not," he agreed. "But that doesn't mean God can't use you right where you are."

I stared at Kyle and swallowed a lump in my throat. "You think God can use *me*?" I looked away from his gaze. "What could I possibly have to offer anyone else?" The words came out in a whisper. A single tear slid down my cheek. Behind it surged an ocean of tears, where I thought my potential, my promise, my dreams, had drowned.

"Linds . . ." Kyle trailed. Could he see the ocean inside? "Lindsey, have you given your heart to the Lord?"

My lip trembled. "I . . . I don't know."

"That's OK, Linds. God loves you. He loves you no matter what you've done." Kyle reached for his Bible. "Would it be OK if we look up some scriptures together?"

"Sure," I mumbled, even though it felt weird. We were two kids who grew up scoffing at our Sabbath School lessons, and now we were going to have a Bible study together.

"Ephesians chapter 1 says He chose you, Linds, before you were even born. He created you because He delighted in you."

The lump in my throat grew.

"God delights in *me*? What did I do to deserve that?"

"Nothing, Linds. There's nothing we can do to make God love us. And nothing we can do to make Him stop loving us. He just loves us because we are His children, and Jesus paid the penalty for us, to bring us back to God."

I sighed. "I know. Ugh. *I know*," I repeated, frustrated. "I've heard that before. I know that Jesus 'paid for my sins' on the cross, but I still feel rotten." I looked Kyle in the eyes. "You don't know how bad I am, Kyle." My voice cracked over the words. Had my brother forgotten what a mess I'd made of my life? "The Bible says I am forgiven, but I don't feel forgiven. I'm still so bad."

"I understand how you feel, Linds. And that's not necessarily a bad thing, to be aware of your sins. It shows you are seeking the Lord." Kyle gave me an encouraging look.

"Anyway," he continued, "it's not good to just say, 'God forgives me,' and then forget about our wrongdoing. We have to keep asking Him for forgiveness on a daily basis, because God is still perfecting us. God says, in Isaiah 1:18, 19, 'Come now, let us settle the matter. . . . Though your sins are like scarlet, they shall be as white as snow; though they are red as crimson, they shall be like wool. If you are willing and obedient, you will eat the good things of the land.' So here it says that being sanctified by the Lord is an active process; it depends on what Jesus did, but it also depends on us *reasoning*, or wrestling it out, with the Lord."

"But Kyle, I feel like I do that. But I don't have peace. How do I have peace about that? How can I know that God still loves me?"

"Read Romans 5:1."

I flipped to the verse and read aloud: " 'Therefore, since we have been justified through faith, we have peace with God through our Lord Jesus Christ.' "

"Faith, Linds," Kyle said. "We can have peace through faith in Jesus. We can believe in Him even if we don't see Him working, and even if we don't feel Him there."

I let out an audible groan. More tears slid down my cheeks. "But it's so hard when I can't feel Him, Kyle! I believe that God is real and His Word has power and He *should* be able to help me . . . but I don't feel the power!" my voice came out whiny. "I just don't understand when it gets better. If God is really that powerful, and if I believe in Him, shouldn't I be a happier person?"

"Lindsey," Kyle put down his Bible. "God is working in you more than you know.

I'm so proud of you for how you have gone back to college and started a new life here in Texas. And sometimes it just takes time. It takes a process of God working on us. I think God is working gradually. Can you see all the needs He's meeting in your life? I mean, you have a husband who is providing for you, you were able to go back to college, you have a good home . . . you have a lot going for you."

Kyle's words sunk in; I felt the truth of those words in that moment, and I sensed that God *was* working, somehow, even if I didn't feel Him. I *did* have a lot to be thankful for, and I cried with that realization.

"I know, I know. You're right. I know God is so good." I gulped and caught my breath. "And I guess He is working on me." More tears streamed out. "I don't know why I'm crying so much!" I threw up my hands helplessly. "I guess it's just because, even though I believe God is good, life is still *so* hard." I tried to laugh but ended up choking on a muffled sob.

"Lindsey, please don't give up!" Kyle said. "Look at what 2 Corinthians 3:18 says: 'And we all, who with unveiled faces contemplate the Lord's glory, are being transformed into his image with ever-increasing glory, which comes from the Lord, who is the Spirit.' You are being transformed, *slowly*, as you submit to the Lord, Linds. And 1 Peter 5:10 says, 'And the God of all grace, who called you to his eternal glory in Christ, after you have suffered a little while, will himself restore you and make you strong, firm and steadfast.' "

I was a goner with my tears now. The promise of being "strong, firm and steadfast" sounded *so good;* I so badly wanted those words to describe me.

"So I believe God is going to restore you, Linds. He's doing that even now. But it took a long time for your depression to build, and it will take time for it to heal." He handed me some tissues. "Do you want a new life in Christ, Linds?"

"Yes," I whispered.

"Are you willing to give your heart to the Lord, Linds?"

"Yes."

"Then let's pray. Dear Lord, thank You for my sister's decision to give her heart to You. Lord, I know You have been working in her life and in her heart to bring her to this decision, even if she can't see it. And I thank You for this. I thank You that You have forgiven her for all her sins, and You are always willing to forgive her when she fails. I pray You will strengthen her, and keep building her faith so she can find peace in You, Lord. I pray You will provide for her needs and help her understand the incredible power and riches You have available to her as she goes forward. It won't always be easy, Lord, but thank You that You can provide all she needs, and make her strong in her faith. In Jesus' name, amen."

At the end of the prayer, I was a soggy heap, exhausted from crying, but I felt better. In that moment, I believed God was doing *something*, even though I didn't *feel* Him. And I began to pray more earnestly: *Lord, let me feel Your presence.* I couldn't give up the notion that if God was big enough to meet my outward, physical needs, He must be big enough to meet my emotional needs. Yes, I was making progress in that I was married and I was pursuing a degree. But there still had to be more to this "new life" thing. So, through what I called my "morning monologues" with God, I pleaded for the Lord to make Himself real to me—in my heart.

* * * * *

During another visit from Kyle, one morning I walked into the living room where Kyle had slept, and I saw him draped over our couch. He had a blanket covering him, his head bent, hands clasped, and he looked like he'd been in that position a long time. Silently, I backed out of the room. *What is he doing?* I wondered, although I knew it must be prayer. I'd never seen anything quite like it, aside from in paintings.

Anytime Kyle visited after that, I tried to catch him in the act, to see if he really prayed like that *every day.* As far as I could tell, he did—for up to a half hour. In later years when we had a house, the telltale sign would be a light streaming from the crack in the doorway at 5:30 or 6:00 A.M.—on holidays. We concluded he was having his prayer and devotions.

I wondered if Bible college had taught him to pray like that. Again, I ached to know the secret to connecting with God.

"I want what you have," I told Kyle. "What do you pray about for so long?"

"Well," Kyle said, "it's like a check-in with God. I check my thoughts with Him, to see if I'm staying in His will. I think back to the day's events and mentally check to see if my actions matched up to doing what I know God wanted me to do. I also pray about the future, ask Him for wisdom. I give Him time to bring anything or anyone to mind that He wants me to deal with. A lot of times, if I'm worried or stressed, during prayer I can lay down those worries at the cross—then I sleep better!"

"Oh . . . OK," I said, not really understanding. I figured this method of prayer was reserved for people like my brother—Bible workers, evangelists, pastors. When he was trained for the ministry, he must've learned this mysterious discipline that had him kneeling and praying for thirty minutes at a time. *Another part of his job,* I thought, frustrated. I thought that if I were in the ministry, I would have time to learn how to do that too, and I'd have time to pray that long every day. Unfortunately, I wasn't. I was just another drone in the rat race, just working a lot of hours at the Nutrition Center and taking an over-full load of literature classes toward my English degree. At the end of the day, I was just another lost college student doing the best she could to figure out some kind of plan.

* * * * *

Lord, what do You want from me? I asked God many times in the final months of my bachelor's degree. As I prepared to graduate, my mind exploded with all my options. I'd spent my senior year accumulating debt and graduation credits. I'd tutored in the writing lab. I'd applied to graduate school on the advice of my advisor. And I'd applied for alternative teaching certification, just in case. I had tried, morning after morning, to hear from God, but my repeated prayers—*Lord, what do You want from me?*—felt completely one-sided.

So far, God had remained silent. And none of my options excited me. *So it will have to come down to one door or the other closing for me to know what to do,* I figured. *Thanks a lot for the help, God.*

Again, I had forgotten about the good things that were happening, and the small steps I was taking. For one, Buc and I finally had a small circle of friends, including Julie and Jarrett. Regularly we got together to watch movies, go out to eat, or play board games. It only bothered me a little that we rarely talked about Christ with our *Christian* friends.

The other good thing was that I'd kicked my purging one night, cold turkey, when Buc heard me from outside the bathroom door. "You've got to stop that!" he yelled. "It's hurting you, and it hurts me." His tone of voice and hard grip when I emerged had frightened the desire to throw up right out of me. Out of respect for Buc, I chose exercise instead to dull the pain. And I got so busy with eighteen-credit semesters and thirty-hour workweeks that I didn't have the energy to be actively depressed anymore.

"Busier people are happier people," Dad spouted when I told him about my schedule.

While I wasn't sure I agreed with Dad, I now knew that busier people at least had less time to be depressed. Now, instead of feeling depressed, I mostly felt stressed. I never had enough time to get everything done.

Lord, I prayed, *please, just open some kind of door. Or close one. If You're not going to talk to me, then just give me something to do. Give me some little corner in Texas to call my own.*

I ended up scoring only two interviews. The first was at the University of Texas at Arlington, where I'd been accepted to graduate school and hoped to work as a teaching assistant. The second was at a rural high school in nearby Rio Vista, Texas. Two weeks after my interview with the graduate school, I received the e-mail: "We're sorry," it said, "but we are looking for a candidate with more experience."

True enough, I thought, closing my email. I didn't have much experience.

A few weeks after that, the high school offered me a job teaching freshman English. Buried in the sticks and at the bottom of the region's pay scale, Rio Vista High could afford to take a chance on me.

So that settles it, huh, Lord?

I headed back to high school to get some experience.

Chapter 18

A Profession to Call My Own

2008–2009

**Truth: "I am certain that God, who began the good work within
you, will continue his work until it is finally finished on the day
when Christ Jesus returns."** —*Philippians 1:6, NLT*

Bare rooms opened into more bare rooms. Blank white walls and white carpet surrounded me. Now I had gained not only four bare walls of a classroom, but all these walls in our new home.

I wandered the rooms in awe. Was this really my house? I basked in the sunlight streaming through picture windows and sliding glass doors and skylights. We'd chosen this house for its open concept, and the light.

Lord, thank You for this, I breathed. I'd graduated college, Buc's job was going well, and we had just moved into the nicest house I'd ever lived in. No cracks between the walls and floors, no rodents, no gas stoves. No upstairs we'd have to shut off in winter. Everything was open and ventilated and well lit. And fully carpeted!

I sat down in the sunroom, connected to our new bedroom, and I imagined what was to come in this house. I pictured quiet mornings in prayer where I might finally hear God's voice. I pictured paint on the walls. I wondered if there might ever be children . . . but I quickly dismissed the thought. Children had always been a painful topic, and anyway, I *did* have children to prepare for, at school.

* * * * *

In August, during one of my "morning monologues" with God, I prayed: "Dear Lord, I'm scared. I think this job will be a turning point in my life. But I know if I don't learn to trust You and have more faith, I could become too stressed to even function. God, please give me guidance, direction, and peace about my new job, because I know it will be trying, and I know to get through it I will need Your power working through me."

As I searched my Bible that morning, I came across a verse Kyle had showed me and paused to consider it again: "I am certain that God, who began the good work within you, will continue his work until it is finally finished on that day when Christ Jesus returns" (Philippians 1:6, NLT).

The thought that God was still working on me was comforting, so I kept reading. A few verses down, I read that the apostle Paul was torn between living and dying for Christ (verse 23). I stopped. I reread the verse. "Really?" I marveled. "You mean the spiritual giant, the apostle Paul, actually wanted to die?" I snorted. "I sure know how that feels."

He went on to write that dying would be better (so he could be with Christ), but he realized that it was more beneficial to those around him for him to live (verse 24).

I stopped and bookmarked my place.

My brow crinkled. "Lord, was that You, just now, speaking to me?"

I wasn't used to finding the Bible relevant to my life. Maybe it was because I hadn't read my Bible much, except for the Old Testament, when I started, time and again, the mammoth task of reading the entire book. Maybe there was more here for me than I thought.

"Maybe," I mused, "this attitude of Paul's is one I need to adopt." I sighed with the weight of the challenge. Many, many times I had wanted to depart life. But now God seemed to be saying it was time for me to mature and face my fears.

"Well, God." I harrumphed. "Maybe You know something I don't. Maybe You're telling me that You can use damaged goods—that maybe You can use even me."

We'll see, I thought, and closed my Bible.

* * * * *

The first day of school arrived. It was show time—time to try and let God use me.

As I slowed and turned in to the circular drive, I noted again a statue of an eagle, my old high school mascot, but now, instead of lush Minnesota grass, I saw the Texas Star on the front of the building. I half expected a tumbleweed to blow across my path. What a different feeling it was to be a new teacher as opposed to a new student, and yet, the experiences were similar.

I checked my watch and checked my hair in the rearview mirror. That day I'd debated whether to wear it up or down, unsure which would look more professional. I'd finally settled for wearing my long hair down, its unruly waves gelled into submission. I'd worn the only dress suit I owned, the same two-piece black blouse and skirt I'd worn just months ago at my job interview.

I thought back through the whirlwind of summer preparations I had made: how I had dusted the room, scraped gum off the desks, vacuumed up live and dead grasshoppers, puzzled over how to hang things on cinderblock walls (a glue gun works best, by the way). I'd started with the room, because I knew that would be easiest. Preparing my curriculum had been tougher; I had no idea how to make a plan for a whole year, much less one week. But now, facing my students was the toughest part altogether.

Seven times that day I stood in front of my classes sporting my black business suit and a surety I did not feel. A measly ten years separated me from my freshmen. By sixth period, I wanted to hide in my storage closet. By the end of the second day, I was sure they had spotted me, the spineless imposter posing as an authority figure. I could tell, from the moment I refused to extend a deadline and one of the boys quipped, "But you're young—you're supposed to be cool," that I was in for a fight. These students were not going to rise to my level of decorum, and I had no idea how to handle their shocking lack of it.

I'd heard a dozen educators tell me to start out strict, not to smile until Christmas, but I couldn't. I'd never been a parent, a boss, or an authority figure, and I felt lost trying to play the part. Since I did not consider myself an authority figure, it's no surprise that my kids didn't either.

By Friday afternoon I was so exhausted I collapsed into bed at 6:00 P.M. and slept until morning. This turned out to be a fitting start for the school year, as the next nine months brought alternating bouts of stress, exhaustion, and tears. Often I woke between 4:00 and 5:00 A.M. with knots in my stomach at having to manage seven classes of hormonal, unpredictable teenagers. I lost weight I wasn't even trying to lose.

In the evenings I left school thankful to have survived one more day, yet already dreading the next. To cope with my stress, I exercised excessively. If before the job I'd thought I had made emotional progress, teaching was now calling forth my darkest demons. Once again, negative thoughts filled my head: *I can't do this, I'm incompetent, I'm too damaged.*

In the early mornings I sought comfort in the Psalms, and I prayed for a deeper experience with God. But there was not enough room in my heart and mind for both Satan's lies and God's truth. While I managed to hold it together on the outside, never once crying in front of my classes, Satan's lies dominated in my mind: *I'm a bad teacher. I don't know what I'm doing. It's my fault the students aren't learning.*

While it was true I didn't know what I was doing, in hindsight, this wasn't my fault. I'd had merely a one-month crash course in teaching before my principal handed me a textbook, with no additional resources, and told me to "have at it." Buried in the book room, and in my mentor teacher's closet, were dozens of ancillary teaching texts, but not until the end of the year did I discover these. No one had thought to show them to me, which left me scrambling to make up my own plans, tests, worksheets, and projects from scratch.

Looking back, I did the best I could with the knowledge I had. Of course my instruction was disconnected from week to week, often only touching the surface of our subject matter—but that was because I was in perpetual survival mode. It was because no one had shown me how to form long-range teaching goals, much less how to effect them.

As it was, I measured my success that first year by exactly one question: Did I fill the entire class period? Sometimes I even failed at that.

I've failed at everything, I thought.

Instead of listening to that voice in my head, I wish I'd listened to the voices of those around me, who could see what I couldn't. My principal, Ms. Sparks, for one, never missed an opportunity to tell me I was doing a great job.

"The kids love you," she would quip at the lunch table. Or, "Your room looks great," when she'd pop her head in my door after school.

One day when I emerged from the copy room, she stopped to straighten the collar of my blouse, reminding me of a mother cheering on her child. Another time, when I alluded to my lack of experience, she offered her own memories of being a green twenty-something teacher.

Unfortunately, her kind words didn't change my mind that I was a failure. By the end of the year, I was ready to slam the door on teaching, but Buc constantly reminded me, "This is a good growing experience." And then I got a contract for a second year.

Wow, I marveled, shocked that they wanted me back. *So maybe God* does *have a plan for me in this job.*

Reluctantly, I resolved to come back for another year.

Chapter 19

Rebirth

2009–2010

Truth: "Therefore, if anyone is in Christ, he is a new creation; old things have passed away; behold, all things have become new."
—2 Corinthians 5:17, NKJV

One week before I started my second year of teaching, Kyle called to tell me Mom had gone off her meds.

"What do we do?" I gasped, barely able to breathe.

"I don't know what we *can* do. I mean, eventually, you know Mom's going to end up in the hospital again."

"And that leaves Caleb without a capable parent . . ." I responded. "There's no way Ray would get custody of him, is there?"

"I don't know," Kyle said.

Then, silence. *What if Mom died?* We both wondered.

Mom had been diagnosed with breast cancer earlier in the year, and in the eight months leading up to that day, Kyle and I, along with Mom's older brother, had urged her to get conventional treatment, to no avail.

After having a lump removed from her breast, Mom had refused conventional treatment; she chose instead to fight her cancer with a whole food diet, juicing, supplements, and vigorous exercise. And that wouldn't have been so scary had she not also decided, just now, to stop conventional treatment for her other "diagnosis."

As Kyle relayed this ugly turn of events to me, my stomach churned. Now that she was off her bipolar medication, there was almost no chance of convincing her to take cancer treatments. No longer did Mom's vacation from her meds just impact her, or us; this time it spelled doom for our little brother. I imagined the worst-case scenario: if she resisted treatment for both conditions, Caleb would be abandoned, at least temporarily, when she went to a mental institution, but possibly permanently if she passed away from cancer.

"Oh, Lord!" I prayed that night, sinking to my knees. "I feel so helpless! What is going to happen to Mom? What's going to happen to Caleb? Is she going to die? Is he going to be left to foster care, or stuck with his drunken dad? God, I am lost right now. I'm so scared!

"Lord, I don't know what to do! I need Your guidance and wisdom—for me, and for the others involved. Please show me what I should be doing. Please give me peace of mind. Help me to 'honor my mother.' Please preserve her until I can see her again, but better yet, heal her, Lord. I don't know what I'll do if something happens to her. I don't know what any of us will do, especially Caleb. Oh, please protect Caleb! Please shield him from this somehow. He shouldn't have to go through this. But I am not there to save him, and I cannot go to him right now. Oh Lord, *help*!"

I cried myself to sleep that night, only to wake every few hours to cry some more. It was only a matter of time before Mom went to the hospital—and only one week until I would go back to school.

* * * * *

This year I'd be teaching juniors instead of freshmen, and I had already decided this year would be better than last. *I will not repeat my first year,* I vowed. To that end, all summer I had been planning, calculating, strategizing, collecting ideas, and gathering resources. While I couldn't predict the kids' behavior, I *could* make sure I had plenty for them to do. This was my battle plan for the school year.

Now, with Mom's situation, that battle plan became even more important. My mantra changed from *I will not repeat my first school year* to *I* cannot *repeat that school year.* Now, with so much on the line, I knew I did not have the emotional reserves to fight two battles. It was simply time to be an adult.

* * * * *

On the eve of the first day of school, Kyle called to say Mom was in the hospital and Caleb was in foster care.

"I'll take him in," Kyle said.

"I'm willing to take him too," I agreed. "If we *can* take him." Now that Caleb was in the care of the state, it was doubtful that Kyle or I, living outside of Minnesota, could take him.

"I can call social services tomorrow," Kyle offered, knowing that it was my first day of school.

I thanked him, and after a few more solemn words, we ended the call.

Then, I collapsed in tears. I slumped to the floor. And I kneeled in prayer, supplicating again for Mom's health and Caleb's safekeeping—and wisdom, guidance, and peace for Kyle and me. "And Lord," I finally sniffled, raising my head to wipe away my tears, "please let the kids be nice to me tomorrow. Please give me a good first day of school."

* * * * *

God answered my prayers, at least the ones regarding school. Despite the stress of the season, I left the high school that first day feeling energized and hopeful.

"Thank You, Lord," I prayed, driving home. "They were awesome! Just awesome! How good You were to me today—how pleasant You want to make this school year for me!"

I was still in disbelief at how smoothly the day had gone, and how truly pleasant this class of kids seemed. From first period all the way through eighth, the day had been a delight. The students ate up my introduction PowerPoint, in which I joked that my name could be pronounced by stringing together the words "gin" and "key": "Just think of opening up a box of gin with a key," I said, gaining confidence with each introduction. The kids bought my new plan to start each student off with his or her own journal. As soon as they walked in the room, I pointed out the colorful composition books on the table: "Pick out a composition book, put your name and the class name in the front cover, and when you are done today, leave your journal in the egg crate labeled with your class period. Every day you will pick up your journal on the way in, and leave it here on the way out."

Finally, I was in my element. This year I would base my instruction on what I knew, and that was personal writing. By the afternoon, I felt confident I was on the right track. Perhaps they could sense the genuine enthusiasm I had not felt one year earlier.

That week, things continued to go well, and even into the second and third weeks, things sailed smoothly, at least at school. My debut unit was not reading a novel, writing an essay, or drilling grammar. Rather, it was a unit on *The Seven Habits of Highly Effective People,* a book Kyle had recommended to me, and the book that had inspired me all summer long. Passing along those praiseworthy habits to my students was part of my plan for circumventing bad behavior, keeping the kids interested, and showing them this class was to be about more than just English. I wanted my class to offer substance and meaning, because that was what I was searching out for myself.

* * * * *

Every night at home, my stress drove me to my knees, and every day at school, for the first few weeks, my lessons reinforced the need to "be proactive" in order to form new habits. During those first weeks of school, the habit I worked on forming was reading my Bible and praying consistently.

I'd made similar efforts before, but this time was different. This time, I wasn't just reading random Bible verses and saying a prayer to check these items off my to-do list. This time, I was genuinely crying out to God for help, and genuinely looking for answers in His Word. To that end, I gave up the idea (for now) of reading the Bible from start to finish, and instead turned to the books that seemed most relatable to me: Psalms, Proverbs, and the entire New Testament.

At this time, I wasn't fully aware of how deeply rooted Satan's lies were in my heart and mind; I just thought I was a negative person, prone to depression. But I did know by this point that I needed to build my foundation on something better than my own understanding (Proverbs 3:5). The Bible says, "All scripture is given by inspiration of God, and is profitable for doctrine, for reproof, for correction, for instruction in righteousness, that the man of God may be complete, thoroughly equipped for every good work" (2 Timothy 3:16, 17, NKJV). I wanted the Bible to be my foundation. I wanted to be "thoroughly equipped for every good work." I desperately did *not* want to continue life as I'd been living it. I didn't want to be so fragile that bad turns, like Mom going off her meds, or a bad class period, incapacitated me. I wanted to become that "new creation" that I read about, and the Bible said I could if I made God's Word my foundation. But I decided it couldn't be my foundation unless it became a part of me. I would need to learn self-discipline.

Studying the Seven Habits helped me to form the habit of self-discipline I needed. By the end of our three-week unit, I could personally attest that three weeks, as Stephen Covey said, was the magic number for habit formation. By the fourth week, I craved my morning Bible and prayer time and wouldn't think of skipping it. Now, I sat down every morning and read the Word for at least fifteen minutes before I left for school. And the Word had a lot to say about self-discipline. Proverbs said, "A person without self-control is like a city with broken-down walls" (25:28, NLT). I didn't want to be that broken-down city, emotionally susceptible to whatever happened around me. Second Timothy said, "For God has not given us a spirit of fear and timidity, but of power, love, and self-discipline" (1:7, NLT). I saw that God's plan was also for me to be proactive (Stephen Covey had not invented this habit . . . God had!). It was godly to be self-disciplined. Psalms told me how I could become more disciplined and fortified against outside forces: "Thy word have I hid in mine heart, that I might not sin against thee" (119:11, KJV). This verse told me that *reading* the Word was not enough; if I wanted changes in behavior, I also had to memorize it.

So I underlined the passages that spoke to me. I wrote them on index cards, and I kept them at the dining table. While I ate breakfast, during my commute, and when I lay in bed, I meditated on those words.

The first passage I memorized was 2 Corinthians 12:9, 10: " 'My grace is sufficient for you, for my power is made perfect in weakness.' Therefore I will boast all the more gladly about my weaknesses, so that Christ's power may rest on me. That is why, for Christ's sake, I delight in weaknesses, in insults, in hardships, in persecutions, in difficulties. For when I am weak, then I am strong." I recited this verse over and over whenever my situation threatened to overwhelm me. When I was tempted to crumple into despair, I spoke the words out loud. "No, Lindsey, my weaknesses, my hardships, my difficulties don't get to determine my emotions. God's Word tells me His power is made perfect in my weakness. I don't have to cry over this; I can rejoice that God is working *in* it, and eventually He will work it *out*."

To be sure, I often didn't know *what* God was doing. I couldn't always see Him working as I blindly followed. But I found it much easier to let God worry about the results than worrying myself. Instead of concentrating on what I could not control—Mom's decisions, Caleb's whereabouts, my students' behavior—I focused on what I *could* control. At the moment, that was being the best teacher I could be, and filling my mind with God's promises. The more I read, the more I realized just how much the Bible had to say to me.

The Bible was all about overturning old habits and harmful patterns in our lives, and that was what I needed to do. When I felt like things would never improve with Mom and Caleb, I could claim these promises: "Weeping may endure for a night, but joy comes in the morning" (Psalm 30:5, NKJV); "We know that all things work together for good to those who love God, to those who are the called according to His purpose" (Romans 8:28, NKJV); and "I consider that our present sufferings are not worth comparing with the glory that will be revealed in us" (verse 18).

When I felt that I could count on nothing staying the same, I could remember, "Jesus Christ is the same yesterday, today, and forever" (Hebrews 13:8) and "God is our refuge and strength, an ever-present help in trouble. Therefore we will not fear, though the earth gives way and the mountains fall into the heart of the sea" (Psalm 46:1, 2).

When I felt worn out, I could imagine Jesus saying, " 'Come to Me, all you who labor and are heavy laden, and I will give you rest' " (Matthew 11:28, NKJV). The rest and peace didn't always come immediately: I read that I needed to "wait" on the Lord, but if I did that, He would strengthen me (Psalm 27:14; Isaiah 40:31). As I memorized and meditated on Scripture, God *did* strengthen me. But He didn't give me enough strength to "just get by." He didn't only deal with me on the outside; He dealt with me on the inside.

I found special encouragement in passages about my thought patterns. I read that my natural mind wanted to steer away from God: "The carnal mind is enmity against God; for it is not subject to the law of God, nor indeed can be" (Romans 8:7, NKJV). I learned that my natural mind wanted to follow the world, but that wasn't God's way: "Be not conformed to this world: but be ye transformed by the renewing of your mind, that ye may prove what is that good, and acceptable, and perfect, will of God" (Romans 12:2, KJV). I learned that my natural mind actually brought death! "Letting your sinful nature control your mind leads to death. But letting the Spirit control your mind leads to life and peace" (Romans 8:6, NLT). How this verse hit me! I remembered so clearly the words, "Life sucks; I want to die," throbbing in my mind. These words had been my mantra for years, and they very nearly *had* killed me! Writing about new life to the Ephesians, Paul said, "You were taught, with regard to your former way of life, to put off your old self, which is being corrupted by its deceitful desires; to be made new in the attitude of your minds; and to put on the new self, created to be like God in true righteousness and holiness" (4:22–24).

How was I to be renewed in the attitude of my mind? I took special note of Philippians 4, which commanded me to "rejoice in the Lord" and pray about everything instead of worrying. If I did these things, the Bible promised that the "peace of God, which transcends all understanding, will guard [my heart]." Isaiah also told me that if I fixed my mind on Him, God would keep me "in perfect peace" (26:3). As I rejoiced in the Lord and took my concerns to Him, not only did God strengthen me, but He also gave me peace.

Yes, God's words changed me . . . from the inside out. For the first time in a long time, I didn't only *look* OK on the outside. I *felt* OK. Today, I like to go back to those happy journal entries where I noted, elated, "Look at me! I actually sound happy! I'm not used to feeling like this!" For the first time since I could remember, I was not depressed. Previously, I was a glass-half-empty kind of girl. Now, I usually saw the glass half full.

Life wasn't all rosy on the outside yet—I didn't know what was going to happen to Mom or Caleb—but as far as my inner peace, it didn't matter. I was on a honeymoon with God, finally getting to know the awesome Father and Provider that He is. Later, when I considered this time in my life, I would think of the well-known poem "Footprints" and marvel at its profundity. So I learned that being a child of God does not mean life is always peachy. He doesn't always change our circumstances when we ask Him to. But when life hurts and doesn't promise to change, God can change *us*—and He always carries us through.

* * * * *

In late September I finally made plans to visit Minnesota, but it wasn't because of Mom. While I was teaching one day, Kyle called to tell me our grandpa had lost his battle with throat cancer. Now, Buc and I, Kyle, and his new wife, Cindi, would return to Minnesota for the funeral. In the back of my mind, I knew we would also have to assess the damage with Mom.

Chapter 20

Home Again

2010–2011

Truth: "Weeping may endure for a night, but joy comes in the morning."   *—Psalm 30:5, NKJV*

*H*ow are you doing?" Buc leaned over the armrest. It was late Saturday night, and our plane was beginning its descent. The lights of Minneapolis twinkled below.

I opened my eyes and rolled my head toward him. "I'm fine; just tired." After Kyle's call a week earlier, we had purchased our tickets, I'd scraped together some lesson plans, and then I had come down with a cold. I'd spent that morning in bed, letting the exhaustion finally wash over me. Now it felt exactly right that I should be sick. I'd been through a lot in the past month, and now my body was telling me to rest.

"I'm sorry again about your grandpa." Buc looked concerned. "Are you sure you're OK?"

I laughed. "Sure, honey. You don't have to worry about me on *that* account. I'm sad that he died, but I was never close to him." Compared with how close Buc had been to *his* grandpa, I was practically a stranger to mine. I knew Buc couldn't understand how little this death affected me. He still sometimes got choked up talking about his late grandpa, but I wasn't sure I would even cry at *my* grandpa's funeral.

"You know, the thing I'm more worried about is going back to Dad's." I didn't need to remind Buc how visits to the old house affected me. Every time I'd gone to Dad's since moving to Texas, I'd always cried for a while because of the memories and emotions associated with the place. And Mom's place would not have been any better except that Caleb kept things lively. Over the years, the tears had decreased, but the house's frozen-in-time aspect always troubled my visits.

"The other thing that worries me is what I'm going to find with Mom . . . if I even get to see her on this trip." We would be staying in Minnesota just four days, and Mom lived two hours north of Dad.

"You can't worry about her, babe. She's an adult, and she has to lie in the bed she made. You've already done plenty. It's time for you to move on and stop letting her problems take you down."

I was touched by his words, even though they were the same ones he'd voiced many times. When I was still a young, depressed bride, when phone calls from parents or visits back home would send me into tears of incapacitation, Buc would get angry on my behalf. He would hold me and listen to me recite, yet again, my life's woes, and he would tell me, "I wish you didn't have to visit there anymore until you could go without being reduced to *this*" (referring to the soggy, crumpled heap I became in his arms at family flashbacks).

"Babe, you're right. I agree with everything you say, but I think I'm doing better. Don't you?"

"Yeah, but you've also been one thousand miles away from this stuff. The real test will be when you walk through your dad's door."

I nodded. I knew he was right.

* * * * *

Four hours later, I entered, Dad and Buc on my heels. I blinked hard. Was this the same house? Houseplants yawned all around me. China and other breakables filled the walls and corners. Doilies dusted the kitchen table, end tables, and floral pink furniture.

"*Wha-a-at . . .*" I couldn't even form a full sentence.

"Place looks a little different, doesn't it?" Dad was amused at my shock.

Buc whistled. "What happened to your bachelor pad, Daryl?"

There were girly lamps, decorative dolls, even a piano. Every inch dripped with a woman's touch.

"Juanita." Dad answered matter-of-factly. "Juanita is what happened."

Juanita was his new significant other, the last in a string of three women he'd dated after Mom. I had met Juanita once, the previous spring break, when she had accompanied Dad to Texas for a visit. Juanita took as much care with her appearance as she did with interior decorating. Blond-haired and blue-eyed, she caught Dad's attention when he saw her working in the local credit union. To woo her, he'd made multiple mix tapes, named them "Juanita Baby, volume 1," "Juanita Baby, volume 2," etc. He didn't stop until he'd made more than twenty tapes, and Juanita agreed to date him. Eventually, he made her more than fifty cassettes.

"What do you think of it?" Buc asked Dad. "Do you like it?"

My mouth hung open.

Dad shrugged. "Oh, it's all right. It's not what I would've done with the place . . ."

"Clearly!" Buc said. They both laughed.

"But it makes her happy." Dad shrugged again. "That's what matters."

"Whoa!" I finally blurted. Before I could form another thought, Kyle and Cindi were standing before me, swallowing up my musings in hugs and greetings and laughter. "Can you believe it?" Kyle asked me. "It's a different house!" In a lowered voice, he added, "Juanita has been good for Dad."

As I curled under fresh-smelling covers that night, I decided Kyle was right, but he'd left something out. Juanita wasn't just good for Dad. She was good for all of us.

* * * * *

On Sunday we dressed up and went to Grandpa's funeral at the same church where my parents had been married. I smiled awkwardly at cousins, aunts, and uncles whom I hadn't talked to in years. I noticed that Grandma was calm, her face unmarred by a single tear, even when the soldiers played "Taps" for this dead World War II vet. As I watched my high school algebra teacher, fully outfitted in soldier garb, pay homage to Grandpa, a funny thing happened: I couldn't stop crying. A few of my relatives dabbed their eyes, but most didn't shed a tear.

My wedding day flashed before my eyes. Today signified another missed opportunity. I would never know Grandpa.

At the reception, I approached Juanita with glassy eyes. "I just wanted to say thank you for everything you've done to the house. I—"

"Oh, honey," she said, seeing my tears. "It's no problem. Are you sure you like it?"

"Oh," I gulped. "More than you know!"

Minutes later, an unexpected visitor showed up.

"Mom!" I exclaimed. I didn't know that that very week she had been discharged from the hospital. Now, she was like a stranger standing before me. Her thick brown hair had grown long, and her body thin. Her cheekbones arched high in her face. *The cancer diet,* I thought. Before, she had told me she was trying to "starve" the cancer with a strict diet of fruits and vegetables. But she looked like she had starved *herself.*

"You look so skinny, Mom." I pulled back from our hug. "Are you getting enough to eat?"

"Oh, yes, I'm eating a ton. I ate almost a pound of blueberries on the way here. The grocery store had a great deal on them." She smiled, then covered her mouth self-consciously. "I don't have any in my teeth, do I?"

I laughed, despite myself. That's when I noticed how bright her eyes looked. She was thin, but she looked healthy. Vigorous, even. Her mind seemed restored. Maybe her body was healing too.

"Buc, Kyle, Cindi, and I are going back to Dad's to eat," I said, frowning at the table of all-meat entrees. "Do you want to join us? Dad's going to be here for a while talking to the relatives and drinking coffee and . . . well, you know Dad.

We're starved; we're going to have some spaghetti. That won't be too awkward for you, will it?"

Mom craned her neck to find Dad. He was engrossed in conversation with his brothers. She nodded. "Sure, if that's OK with him."

"Oh, Dad won't care." I waved my hands. One of the best qualities about Dad was his ability to move on with life, even if it meant hosting his ex-wife.

"Hey, did you drive that pickup?" I pointed at a teal-colored truck beside the curb.

"Yep, that's my ride. It's even a stick shift."

"Where on earth did you get it?"

"Oh, that's one of Dean's trucks. He didn't think my car was safe."

Dean was Mom's new boyfriend, and the man who had finally replaced Ray. She'd met him around the same time Dad met Juanita, when she started caring for Dean's aged mother. As the story went, Dean was attracted to the loving way she treated his mother, so he asked her out. This truck was one of the many Dean had plucked from his scrap metal business. Later, Mom would tell me she was attracted to Dean because he had stood in her corner as she battled her various health challenges. While her whole family told her to get conventional treatment for her cancer, Dean brought her bags of carrots to juice. When Mom was committed to the mental hospital, Dean stood at the front desk and bartered with the nurses to give her back her own clothes, and her dignity.

"Mom looks good," I remarked to Buc on our way out of the church. We watched her climb into the truck.

"She looks funny driving that old gas guzzler," Buc said.

"I don't know . . ." I said, considering how the vehicle swallowed her. Mom never would have driven a vehicle like that when I lived with her. A bookworm like me, she also would not have crunched numbers as a fill-in bookkeeper at a scrap metal shop.

After a moment I said, "I think it works."

Buc gave me a funny look. "You do?"

"Yeah. I think it says she's a fighter."

* * * * *

At Dad's, the five of us sat around the kitchen table heaping our plates with spaghetti.

"Do you think you made enough, Linds?" Kyle asked, gesturing at the brimming pot of pasta.

"Oh, I know!" Buc said. "She always does this! She always makes way too much!"

"Hey," I said, shrugging. "I'd rather have too much than not enough."

"Well, you didn't have to feed an army."

"I was hungry, and it's hard to estimate uncooked spaghetti. Lay off!"

We were all hungry. The fare at the funeral reception, mostly meats and sweets, didn't jibe well with our vegetarian diet, or Mom's cancer diet. It didn't help that Dad didn't keep much food in his pantry. He always said he didn't know how to cook for his kids anymore, now that we were vegetarians. Dad had maintained his Midwestern meat-and-potatoes diet (minus the unclean meats), and because of that, we'd been hungry since arriving at Dad's. This meal had been born out of necessity, Buc and me dashing to the store after the funeral.

Later the meal would become a running joke between the five of us, how Dad ended up eating spaghetti for the rest of the week because he couldn't stand to waste food. It was the beginning of many long-overdue laughs we would finally share as a family.

* * * * *

Back in Texas, I felt light. Mom's cancer was in remission, and she was back on track with her meds. Dad was happily matched up with Juanita; and Caleb was soon released from foster care, taking with him a beloved new companion, a dog named Wilbur. I was still gleaning encouragement from the Bible each day—but now even the world around me gave me peace.

Although we had been married for four years, Buc and I had never owned a Christmas tree. I had never wanted one because holidays reminded me of my broken family. But this year, an unfamiliar, almost ecstatic feeling seized me. I wanted to put up a Christmas tree! On October 10, we did. Meanwhile, at school a similar urge seized me. I wanted to decorate!

When I draped my classroom in harvest decorations, it was very uncharacteristic of me, this woman who didn't want a wedding, and my students noticed. The day they walked in to see scarecrows, orange and brown wreaths, bouquets, and chalkboard runners, their eyes bulged. In their journals that day, several wrote about how these small touches made them feel warm inside and ready for fall. I, too, was ready to move on.

Three days before Christmas, I wrote the following in my journal:

No matter what happens, praise be to God for His loving care all these years. I can't believe how much I've grown spiritually, in the last few. I'm so glad to be a believer; I think life would be absolutely dismal without the hope God gives us. And I've been already very touched this Christmas season—anytime I hear Christmas songs on the radio or hear a Christmas message—with the meaning of the season.

It's kind of struck me anew—perhaps for the first time—of what an act of love Jesus' coming was. "Joy to the world!" Those lyrics alone have made me teary-eyed. What a joy it is to this dreary world to know that our Savior came just for us. Dismal doom suddenly turned into resounding joy with the promise of Christ's second coming. I feel so joyful today and this season for my wonderful hope, my Christian faith.

I still have some growing to do as far as sharing my faith with others. I'm usually too timid to break that sort of ice with others, but God does miracles all the time. Surely He will eventually use me to spread that joy.

God had answered so many prayers—indeed, as Kyle had said years before, He'd been answering them all along—but only now did I see it. Most recently, I had been praying every day on my commute that my family—my whole family—could spend Christmas with us . . . and they were going to!

At Buc's skillful persuasion, both of my parents and Kyle and Cindi all agreed to stay in our house for Christmas. My heart overflowed to have all of us gathered in one place. Where we were tense, Buc, Dad, and Caleb lightened us up.

When there was an awkward silence, Caleb filled it with the rambunctious energy of a ten-year-old. He made us laugh with his attempts to make friends with the dog in our yard, Teddy (we were keeping Teddy for a friend at the time); and he impressed us with his drawing skills, YouTube videos he had filmed and posted of Thomas the Train, and his big vocabulary—showing off words like *curmudgeon, colossal, skeptical,* and *dubious.* What a breath of fresh air Caleb was! So much life in my little brother. Up until then, I had worried about how he was doing; but this visit was proof that even after all he'd been through, he was a well-adjusted, gifted kid.

Overall, the lighter mood was palpable, like when Dad gave an ugly, multi-colored, green-striped shirt to Buc. A friend had given him that shirt among a mess of other clothes, but it was practically un-wearable because it was so ugly. Dad saw it and thought of Buc. The rest of us erupted in laughter at Buc's reaction, and his threat, "I'll get you back, Daryl." Ever since, the notorious green shirt has been passed back and forth at Christmastime, or stuffed into a suitcase when visits end. The shirt is still in limbo today. It became the icebreaker my family needed for visits; it became a symbol of moving on with life, which I realized we were all doing in our own ways.

Four months after Christmas, Dad and Juanita wed at a marriage mill in South Dakota, and within two years, Mom and Dean tied the knot as well. Kyle and Cindi decided to become long-term missionaries to Thailand, but before they left, Buc and I got to spend several weekends with them: one of them on a road trip to Minnesota for Mom and Dean's reception; another, a surprise visit to Arkansas for Kyle's thirtieth birthday. The final visit was a week spent in Texas, during which the four of us went river tubing, visited a Dead Sea Scrolls exhibit, drove through the Fossil Rim Animal Park, and played doubles ping pong in our living room. Finally, it felt like we had our lives back.

* * * * *

During my third year of teaching, I applied again for graduate school. My teaching stint had helped me figure out that I wanted the freedom of a college classroom to teach what and how *I* wanted to teach. No more state tests, no more pep rallies, no more parent phone calls. I had visions of leisurely days in my office where I would prepare my curriculum. I would still be creative with my assignments, like I had been at the high school, but now I would also be free to include the Bible and other Christian literature. At college, I would have my students write on topics that could help them personally, not just academically. And with the relaxed teaching schedule of college, as opposed to the eight periods crammed into one high school day, I might even find time to write a bit myself. So, I put in my resignation and I packed up my things.

On the last day of school, as I sat gazing at bare walls and boxes of lessons, files, and projects that I would soon stow, I remembered those words that had sent me there (and not to graduate school) in the first place: "You need more experience." I knew I'd gotten more than I'd come for.

As students stopped by my door that day, showering me with hugs, cards, gifts, and words of thanks, I marveled at how God had changed me through three years of teaching—and apparently used me right where I was.

Part 3—Uprooting, Replanting

When you experience a loss, you have to grieve for it before you can let it go. That seems to be common knowledge in the case of death. But I think it applies to other losses too. Like the loss of one's family by divorce and distance and remarriage—the loss of traditions and that familiar and comforting sense of "coming home." I think this is a loss that both my older brother and I have struggled to articulate over the years. Now I am articulating it because I am serious about finally healing from it.

The more I let this out, the more room I'm finding in my heart for my family members, new and old. Bitterness for the Gendkes' happiness and hominess is giving way to love and the realization that I, too, can participate in their—our—family, if I will speak up and let my voice be heard. With that realization has also come compassion for my own parents who—though I felt may have underappreciated and undervalued me—truth be told, I'm sure just never realized how I was feeling. I need to forgive them for they "knew not" what they did, or didn't do.

So I've come to this conclusion. My family is not at fault for not understanding me. That's because I've barely spoken up in these last eight years. If the fault lies with anyone, it lies with me, for bottling myself and my feelings. It's time to speak up. And if they don't appreciate me doing that, well, nothing will have been lost. But if they actually like what I have to say, I have everything to gain—sisters, brothers, mom, and dad. Sounds good to me. This healing thing—writing to my roots—is pretty great, you know?

—from my "Writing to My Roots" notebooks, October 2012

Chapter 21

Old, Bad Fruit

2011

Lie: I'm past my pain; I don't have to deal with it anymore.

Truth: "People lie; patterns don't." — Paul Coneff (see Luke 6:43–45)

God gives a special gift when life slows down—when jobs are stopped or plans paused. In these times, God can make things clear that we otherwise wouldn't see: He shows us what's inside of us, and gives us the choice to ask His help or not.

For so many years, I had tried to avoid having free space and time, because free space brought time to think, and thinking brought pain. But by age twenty-six, a lot had changed. *I* had changed in many ways, and now I wasn't scared of the quiet, and now I had carved out the next six to eight years of relatively "quiet" time to earn my doctorate. I wasn't scared of being alone with myself because I didn't think there was anything left to be scared of. I didn't want to die; I didn't want to binge and purge; and better yet, I even had some goals.

While many of my peers proceeded to fill up their homes and lives with children, I proceeded to fill up my life with everything but. I began graduate school full time. I started a young adult Bible study in our living room to witness to my friends. And at church I became head of communications and head of the music committee.

Because I had a plan for my life now, I wasn't scared of all that alone time I would have, in the library, or at home, or in the car, commuting the almost-hour to the graduate school several times a week. Not living on or near campus, and not working, graduate school would be a very solitary pursuit, but I didn't quite grasp how solitary, how quiet it would be. And I didn't anticipate how all this quiet would shake me to my core and leave me searching once again for answers.

* * * * *

I felt the ache around the edges of Christmastime.

Buc and I were driving to my niece's fall festival at school, a fundraising event loaded with booths of baked goods, games, a silent auction, and lots of bodies in a gymnasium. I was continuing a conversation I'd been having with my hubby for more than a week about how I just didn't really *know* people in my life, mainly those at my church. But that day, as we drove onward to meet up with my in-laws, I got to thinking about *them,* and how I didn't really know *them.* And to my surprise, I heard myself telling Buc I'd like to know my mother-in-law better.

But I wasn't sure how.

So, instead, I did what I always did. I complained to Buc.

"So, how many gifts do you think she'll get all the kids this year?" I sniffed, feeling the old walls go up.

"Ugh-h-h," he groaned. "Are you starting that again? You need to give that a break!"

I prickled in self-defense. "I'm just saying. There are always so many gifts at Christmas."

"Yes," Buc said, exasperated. "But that's just Mom."

My eyes rolled. "I know. And after all these years, I *still* don't understand her. I mean, it never ceases to amaze me how spoiled these kids are."

Buc tried to interrupt me: "You're still bitter about your own family and how you guys don't *have* any real Christmas traditions anymore."

But I plowed on. "I'm not talking about my family right now," I snapped. "I'm just saying, too many gifts leaves no *time* or *space* to think about what it really means to give and receive.

"And how unique and special are gifts if you get someone so many? Doesn't quality have to go down? And what about practicality? How could it be possible that kids *need* all this stuff? It's impossible. And for that matter, is it feasible that they will *use* all that stuff? Do you realize that the kids go home with trash bags full of gifts, and that's probably where a lot of those gifts end up—in the trash?"

"Stop!" Buc finally shouted, jarring me into silence. "You need to just stop, and get over yourself!" He exhaled with palpable disgust. "Maybe I don't agree with it either, but it's my mom. It's what she does. And if you weren't so bitter about your own family, you could see that she's just doing it out of love. It makes her feel good. So let it go. I'm done with this."

I sat stunned, like a little kid who had just been spanked. His words stung. My pride hurt. And so did my heart. Initially, I felt angry at Buc for treating me like a child, but as the day wore on, as I watched Margie laughingly and lovingly interact at the festival with her grandchildren, and with other children—she and Mike were frying corn dogs to help raise funds, as they had done so often—my heart softened a little. Maybe I *was* wrong. Maybe Buc had a right to call me out on my childish behavior. Because, I had to admit, I *was* sounding like a child.

Over the next few days as I thought and prayed some more about Margie and my disdain for Christmas, I sensed I was perhaps confusing issues. So what if I didn't like how my mother-in-law handled Christmas? Why should that bother me so much . . . unless I still had issues with my own family?

* * * * *

One morning in early January, I woke at 4:00 A.M. unable to fall back to sleep. I had been dreaming of my parents, after talking to both of them on the phone the previous night. It had been seven months since I'd seen them. And now, I had emptiness in my gut and confusion in my heart.

Why don't my parents come and visit me? I wondered.

We had all watched the days of December slide by, making dismissive comments about how it just wasn't going to work out this year. We had all said that—except Caleb, who had begged Mom to take a bus here. But why had we said it, I now wondered?

How could we have had such a great Christmas the previous year and hardly talk this year?

I started trying to cook up a plan to get myself from Texas to Minnesota that winter. *I'll give in,* I decided. *I'll* drive. *I'll* be the one to travel. *Just let me go home, pretend to go home, for a while. Just let this emptiness stop.*

And then, as soon as those thoughts hit, more thoughts seeped through: *Why is it always* me *trying? Why does it feel like it's always been* me *making these efforts?*

And something else—some anger that was directed at myself as much as at anyone else. Why couldn't my family be honest and tell each other we missed one another? On the phone the previous night with both my parents, I had thought of telling them I wanted to visit—that I missed them. But I had dismissed those thoughts. And they hadn't gotten to hear them. As I sat wide awake at 4:30 A.M., I wondered, *Why do I do that?*

Why don't I tell them how I feel? Why don't I ask them to visit more?

I knew I didn't speak up because I didn't want to make my parents feel worse than they already might about not much. It *was* a hardship to visit, money- and time-wise. But . . . I was their child. Wasn't I worth it?

* * * * *

The emptiness started chasing me in earnest after Christmas break. It was the emptiness of not having my family around, not being close with my Texas family, and not being connected with many friends. But I couldn't see what the real problem was. Or I refused to see it. These emotions that were surfacing—loneliness, anger, resentment, bitterness—were rooted deep in my heart, and I had worked hard to keep them there. I didn't know how to deal with them in a productive way; in the past, they had only led to bitter conversations with Buc, angry journal entries, or painful tears. So now, I simply tried not to deal with them. I tried to bury my pain with busyness, with church activities, with career planning. I tried to find meaning in life, and in myself, by the things *I* could do; I wanted to find meaning apart from others because I had learned I couldn't count on others.

On some level I realized what I was doing. I realized that my plans for a grand career and a thriving ministry were not just to benefit my future students and friends. Yes, I wanted to help others . . . but only as long as I could protect myself from getting hurt again.

As I told Buc one afternoon, after we had visited our friends and their new-born baby, I felt a career was a safer investment than kids.

He looked at me like I was deranged. "What?"

"No, no, it sounds weird, and maybe I'm messed up, but it makes sense. See, it's safer because you could easily lose your kids—anything could happen to take them away from you in an instant. All your time and effort could be instantly lost, and you can't get them back. But with a career, or a degree, or job experience, nothing can take those away from me. Bad stuff could happen—I could lose my job—but still, nobody can take away that degree or the experience that I have. They're always mine to keep, and I can always, barring severe physical trauma, put them to use again. No one can take them away."

Buc didn't agree.

I knew I was protecting myself, but what I didn't realize was that I was cooperating with Satan. I had swallowed the lie that I could take care of myself. And in doing so, I was following his plan, not mine. His plan was for me to cover up my pain and avoid healing.

But no matter what lies we swallow to cover our pain, that pain will always surface, some way, somehow. As John Townsend has said, "Buried pain is always buried alive."[1] When I faced the silence and quiet of my new life as a non-working, off-campus, full-time college student, conditions were ripe for old, buried roots to pop up.

It didn't help that my public university discounted my Christian faith. It didn't help that my menu of reading and writing asked me to suspend my beliefs and deconstruct all things I had come to hold dear: God, Truth (with a capital *T*), traditional marriage, and the traditional family structure. How could I happily and blindly follow this agenda that asked me to disbelieve the very things I had come to trust in?

As a Christian teacher, I wanted to contribute answers in a difficult world, not raise more questions. But in graduate school, the engine driving all discourse was deconstruction: we deconstructed everything from literary theme to authorial intent to societal structures. We questioned everything. There was no ultimate Truth (with a capital *T*) because, in grad school, "truth" was relative. For someone who had found God, what good were these alternate theories?

Suddenly, I felt lost. Again.

Oh God, I prayed. *How can I take this?* Literally, *How will I be able to **use** this education—and another five or six years of it, no less—to inform any of my life goals? Teaching composition from the seat of Christian values. Witnessing to my friends. Being a good wife to Buc. What in the world am I doing here, God?*

As the semester wore on, I became deeply unhappy.

I found myself watching the clock, waiting for my classes to end.

I found myself hating Freud and Foucault and Faulkner, wanting to crawl into a cave and disappear.

I found myself wandering around campus, ducking into bathrooms to cry.

Finally, I found myself at a mental health screening, and a few weeks later, in a counselor's office.

"What brings you in?" Bruce, a middle-aged man wearing Converse sneakers and thick-rimmed glasses, asked. He sat poised, pen in hand.

"I don't know what to do with my life." I tried to sound calm. Inside, I was screaming: *I'm almost thirty, for goodness' sake, I've been married for seven years, and now, all over again, just like some of the college freshmen around me, I don't know what to do with my life. But how could this be?*

I tried to confine the discussion to career, but Bruce kept asking me questions about my home life, my marriage, even my broken childhood.

"I'm sorry," I blubbered, dabbing my eyes with a tissue. "I didn't plan to go there. It's not a big deal anymore. I really just came here to talk about my career."

"Please don't apologize," he said. "Obviously, there's still pain there; it looks like there's still some healing you need to do."

I swallowed a lump in my throat, wanting to ignore this theme that kept surfacing. But Bruce wanted to pursue it.

"How's your relationship with your husband?"

I crinkled my brow. "It's fine; it's really good, in fact."

"Then why do you look like you're about to cry?" Bruce asked softly.

I looked down, embarrassed. "I feel somehow afraid; like it's too good; like it won't last."

What if something happens to him? a voice whispered in my head. *Look how pathetic my life is. I'm sitting here playing "cute little college student" on Buc's dime—on Buc's support, encouragement, love—but I'd be nowhere without him. I'd have nothing without him. I am nothing without him.*

I was surprised at how forcefully my next words came. "Buc could die suddenly, leaving me all alone. And then what would I do?" I stared at Bruce, wondering if he could feel the agony in my question.

"How would I support myself?" I added, tears finally spilling.

Bruce handed me a box of tissues and waited while I blew my nose. Then, he looked me squarely in the face and asked, "Have you seen *Sister Act 2*? Do you remember that line, 'What is it you think about as soon as you wake up in the morning? What can you never get out of your head?' "

The change of subject jolted me.

"That's easy," I answered. "Writing. Writing is what I dream about doing every day." I sighed. "But that's not a valid career plan, is it? I need to have a guaranteed income, and writing doesn't come with any guarantees." I sighed again. "So what am I supposed to *do*?"

Bruce's next words baffled me. "Have you considered *why* you keep having this desire to write?" he asked with kind eyes. "Who do you think put it there?"

Who indeed? I wondered. *Is God calling me to write?* The thought was exhilarating, and also puzzling. What would I write about? In the past, I mostly wrote about my depression and depressing thoughts. Surely I couldn't serve God by continuing in the same vein, but then I felt depressed again! What did I have to do to emerge from this funk, to feel happy again, to find God again?

I went home and called Kyle.

"What's wrong, Linds?" Kyle asked, hearing my sniffles.

"Maybe I'm just lonely," I continued. "Buc is gone this week, and I've come to realize that I really don't like an empty house. The two of us are not enough to fill it, sometimes. Maybe I have a hole for some [sniff] . . ."

"What, Linds?" Kyle asked.

Again I couldn't say it.

"Are you OK, Linds?"

"*Ugh-h-h* . . . [sniff, sniff]. I don't know how to talk to him, Kyle. I can't tell him how I hate grad school. And how I think I'm supposed to do something else. I can't change my mind *again*. But I really don't think the scholarly life is what I want. This indecision is literally making me sick. That's why I went to see a campus counselor."

After a thoughtful moment, Kyle answered. "I would be cautious about going to a secular counselor. He's coming from a whole different paradigm, and his advice won't necessarily be based on God's plan. He's probably not getting at the root of the problem, just treating the fruit."

"What do you mean?"

"Well, God wants to heal every part of us . . ."

My ears perked up at that word *heal*.

"Whoa, wait a minute, Kyle," I interrupted. "What are we really talking about here? I'm talking about choosing my career, and you seem to be talking about some kind of healing. I don't see how the two are related."

"Sure," Kyle said. "Let me explain. To use a personal example, I've felt for a long time that I have to go around looking all put-together, as if there's nothing wrong with me. Well, I had a lot of emotional scars to deal with—you know, from what happened with Mom and Dad—but I've had a hard time letting people in. I never wanted to be vulnerable with others. But if you look at the disciples, God was able to use them because they were humble. It's not God's plan that we hide who we are and put up a false front."

"OK . . . so are you suggesting that I need more healing? And that it is impacting my career choice?"

"Exactly. A lot of times we want to try everything but what we most need to do. We talk to everyone except the One who can most help us." He paused. "Linds, have you brought your concerns to the Lord?"

I prickled at this question. "Yes, I pray every day. I have a devotional every day too," I added, curtly. Was he even listening to me?

Kyle's voice got soft. "There are things buried in people, Linds, and they cover them up with outward stuff—behaviors or habits or addictions. Even careers. *Lots* of people have buried issues they still need to deal with. I covered up my stuff with my accomplishments, and with trying to look OK on the outside." After another pause, Kyle added, "Do you have someone you feel comfortable praying with, Linds?"

I winced at the question. I thought of my friends from Bible study, whose prayer requests never went below skin deep. "No. I don't."

Kyle must be wrong, I decided. There couldn't be something *else* wrong with me.

But as tearful days and weeks wore on, I couldn't deny that something *was* wrong.

Maybe I *did* have some kind of—ugh—"healing" to do, but if God wanted me to tap some deep "root," I told Him He'd have to send a sign. A really clear sign.

---

1. This quote came from a seminar Mr. Townsend gave many years ago in California; my co-author from *The Hidden Half of the Gospel,* Paul Coneff, shared it with me.

Chapter 22

Learning How to Pray

Spring 2012

Truth: "Be still, and know that I am God." — Psalm 46:10

As the spring wore on, I longed to pursue writing and not the PhD. But I felt I needed permission somehow. I needed some validation that this was what I was supposed to do. I needed to know that writing could be different than it was before. And I also needed peace from all the demons that had been bubbling to the surface.

That's when I met Paul Coneff.

Paul came to my church to facilitate a Week of Prayer at the same time I was feeling desperate about my career plans.

Buc and I sat midway up the aisle as lights dimmed for the presentation. With weary eyes, I watched our guest speaker, tall and thin, wearing khaki pants and a matching khaki shirt, fumble with his microphone. Behind him, the screen flashed with a picture of an arrow striking the middle of a heart, and the words "Straight 2 the Heart." I furrowed my brow. The logo looked familiar.

"Why is it," Paul began, "that so many Christians who have accepted the 'good news' of Christ still are not free?" He let the question sink in for a moment.

I felt something stir inside me. I had accepted the "good news" of Jesus, or so I thought, but these days, I didn't feel free.

"Everywhere I go," Paul continued, "including Christian schools and churches, I see addictions, divorce, depression, abuse. It doesn't matter where I go; these problems are everywhere. But when you run into a teenager who's cutting, or a person who's suicidal, what kind of a gospel can you offer that person?" Paul looked intently into the audience.

Wow, I thought. This sounded all too familiar.

"Here's what happens. We lead someone to Jesus Christ, we give them Bible studies, we lead them into the church; and after they get baptized, they're struggling with alcohol or pornography or depression, and they know that it's bad and pray about it; they confess their sin. I call this the cycle of sin-and-forgiveness. But if they don't deal with it, guess what?"

Paul waited for someone to answer: "They sin again," a voice called.

"Let's think for example about a woman who was molested thirty years ago. Now she hates men and is overeating to compensate for the emptiness in her life. By the way, being unloved, or being neglected, can feel as bad as being abused. So, what good is it to tell this woman that Jesus died for her sins and rose again? She already knows that, and she's still living in fear and hate and a cycle of over-eating. What can we offer her?"

As Paul talked on, my negative thoughts surged in my head: *I'm a failure. I can't do anything by myself. I'm a dead weight. My stable life could crumble at any minute. I have to protect myself.*

"See, we can paper over lies with truth for a while. We can cover up our sins and our struggles for a while. But if we don't cut down the tree at the roots, like Ellen White says, then we're not really going to change. We're still going to pro-duce those negative fruits of anger, addiction, cutting, depression, or whatever the case may be. We're not really going to get freedom, or the new life that Christ promises."

I couldn't believe it. Paul was using the same language Kyle had used!

It was then that I realized the connection: Paul had taught at Amazing Facts the same year my brother was there! And the logo Paul had displayed was the same one Kyle had shown me on a prayer card.

"So how do we get new life? First, we have to deal with Satan's lies. We have to deal with that root system that Satan plants in us. As long as the root system is intact, that fruit will keep popping up."

OK, God. I get it. Here's my sign. I prayed. *So, what's next? What do I do with this information?*

When Paul made a call later that week for three men and three women to form a prayer group, I didn't hesitate. I signed up to become part of the Straight 2 the Heart prayer team at my church. In this group, Paul explained, we would not only receive prayer and healing for our own negative roots, but we would be trained to pray with others about *theirs.*

OK again, God, I prayed a second time, marveling at His direct answer to my prayer. *If You say so, then I will trust You. Let's do this, God. Let's get down to my roots.*

* * * * *

Paul spent the next four months instructing a group of five, praying with us and training us to pray with others. These were not quick, clean, thirty-second prayers. They were recursive prayers, messy prayers, prayers that asked Jesus to identify our negative roots and then helped us connect our stories to Jesus' story of suffering. It didn't end there. We delved deeper, praying, "Lord, what else do You want me to know about these roots in my life? What barriers are there in these areas?" Always by the end of the prayer sessions, which dredged up long-buried hurts and often tears, the Holy Spirit revealed blessings, too. He always brought to mind His promises to combat the negative thoughts and painful memories our praying churned up.

What was the purpose of these messy prayers? It was to make "disciples" of us, Paul said. And I couldn't help but notice how that word "disciple" fit so well. We met in each other's homes week after week. We sprawled in a circle on couches or plastic chairs to talk and train and pray, and we shared meals together. Indeed, we functioned a lot like the first disciples.

For our first prayer session, a pre-training session, I sat in a circle at Paul Coneff's house, along with Amanda, my friend from Bible study, and Mary, the women's ministries leader at church. The others would join us later. The three of us sat in an open room at the back of Paul's house in plastic chairs, surrounded by Paul's desk, binders on the floor, stacks of papers on every available surface, and exercise equipment. Burgundy curtains billowed in the breeze of an overhead fan, and a jug of water and some plastic cups sat on a nearby chair. "Help yourselves," Paul told us as he bustled around, punching holes in papers for our training binders. I was again struck by how down-to-earth Paul was, inviting us into his own home, letting us see his mess, and working so closely with his "disciples."

The prayer process, like Paul's approach, is pretty simple, with just three steps:

1. The facilitator asks what the person would like prayer for, with a focus on identifying key negative thoughts (or roots).
2. The facilitator shares Jesus' story of suffering and asks the Holy Spirit to show the person where Christ can identify.
3. The facilitator puts the two stories together in a prayer. Then, we watch the "simple but supernatural" story of Jesus, and the Holy Spirit, do its work, as the facilitator continues to pray for related blessings for the person, as well as ask if there are any barriers keeping the person from receiving those blessings.

* * * * *

"OK." Yvette looked at me on the second day, after both Mary and Amanda had received prayer the night before. Yvette was Paul's assistant and also a new "disciple" being trained in the prayer process. Just a few steps ahead of us in her training, this weekend she was our facilitator. "I've written down your words into a prayer. Would you like to repeat after me?"

"OK," I said. *Now it's my turn to cry,* I thought.

I bowed my head obediently, and we prayed.

Dear Jesus,

Thank You for choosing to fulfill prophecy by struggling to surrender Your will in the Garden of Gethsemane; and thank You for being abandoned, betrayed, and rejected, so You could suffer in Your soul, die for me, embrace all of my struggles, and rise again to heal my wounded heart. Thank You for setting me free from worrying about my future, having to be in control, and feeling I have to try harder and do more, as I receive my true identity as Your daughter.

In Jesus' name, amen.

"Dear Jesus," Yvette prayed next, "thank You for identifying with Lindsey. Are there any blessings or barriers You want to bring to her mind in this area of her life?"

I kept my head bowed, listening for the Holy Spirit, as Paul had instructed us to do.

"That's strange," I said out loud. "I'm seeing a picture of my planner."

"Dear Lord Jesus," Yvette prayed, "what do you want Lindsey to know about her planner, or what messages do You have for her that relates to her planner?"

"I hear a Bible verse," I said after another moment of silence. " 'For I know the plans I have for you,' declares the LORD, . . . 'plans to give you hope and a future.' "

"Ah," Yvette murmured. "That's definitely a blessing!"

I paused to mull that over. "Yeah," I said. "That's a pretty fitting verse, since I'm stressing over my career plans."

"Let's pray again," Yvette said, and we bowed our heads. "Dear Jesus, thank You for the blessing You gave Lindsey, that You know Your plans for her. Are there any barriers keeping Lindsey from receiving the fullness of Your blessing?"

I closed my eyes, and this time a sense of darkness descended on me, a feeling of being cut off from help and hope.

"Is anything coming up?" Yvette asked.

I drew in a shaky breath, not trusting myself to speak. Pictures were flashing through my mind of that dingy apartment where I'd lived after my suicide attempt. Suddenly, I was once again a suicidal college dropout living alone. I felt again the emotions that had led to self-harm. I shivered, tears building behind my eyelids.

"I—I don't know," I stuttered. "I saw something—it was a flashback from about eight years ago. I was back in this single apartment where I lived after . . ." I sniffled, "I lived there after I tried to kill myself."

Amanda handed me the box of Kleenex she'd used the night before. She flashed a sympathetic smile.

"Thanks," I sniffed, wiping my eyes.

Everyone kept still, watching for my reaction. Yvette's pen hung suspended over her notebook.

I shrugged helplessly. "I don't know why I'm having that flashback." *What am I supposed to do with that, Lord? I don't feel the same way I felt back then.*

Or do I? A voice whispered in my ear. I frowned in concentration. My head hurt from thinking, from trying to find the connection. *What's significant about that time in my life?* I wondered. *In 2004, I was a college dropout, failed suicide, hopeless. Today, I am a relatively successful young woman struggling to figure out my next steps . . . struggling* really hard *to figure out my plans . . .*

My inner dialogue stopped at the word *plans.* "For I know the plans I have for you," I heard again.

Suddenly, I gasped.

"I had no plans," I blurted. "That's the connection. At that time, when I was so depressed, the worst thing about my life was that I had no plans. Everything had shattered for me, and all my hopes had fallen through."

There's no purpose to my life, there are no plans for me, I heard an old voice echo.

I stiffened, listening more closely.

I have no plans. My life has no purpose. I can't do anything on my own; I'm pathetic, I'm helpless.

I looked up, stunned. A switch had tripped in my brain. I had heard that voice before, but I had always thought it came from myself. But it didn't! It came from Satan! And all my negative thoughts? They were lies from the enemy of my soul, just as Paul had said.

How can these thoughts still be in there? I had asked myself recently. *How can they still be there after I've received so much Bible truth? After God has given me a "new life"?*

Now I knew how these lies could still be there. I had not allowed God to up-root them. I had received a lot of truth, and that was good, but it wasn't enough. I had participated in what Paul called "beach ball theology." I had tried to push down my negative thoughts, not knowing they were lies from Satan. But like a beach ball being pushed underwater, these thoughts were bound to keep coming up. It was not enough to "paper over lies with truth," Paul had said, because the lies will always come back. For moments that felt like hours, I sat crying in that plastic chair, humbled and awed at what God had brought to me.

"Let's pray again," Yvette said. "Lord, are there any blessings You have for Lindsey as she is hearing these old lies from Satan?"

I bowed my head again, and now, like sweet music to the soul, I heard another voice speaking. It was the voice of the Holy Spirit, the voice of truth.

"Lindsey, you are worried about so many things, things that you don't need to worry about. You are so afraid to let go of control, because you are afraid to return to the despair you felt eight years ago. And I understand. You have tried to handle things on your own, because it's hard for you to trust others. You have tried to make plans in your own wisdom, to prevent future disasters—that's why your planner is so important to you, and that's why having a career is so important. And there's nothing wrong with wanting to feel secure. And there's nothing wrong with planning, or wanting a career.

"But Lindsey, you need to find your security in Me. Not in anything you do or plan. I already have plans for you, and I have glorious, unlimited resources for you to draw upon. My strength is perfect in your weakness—My strength, Lindsey, not your husband's strength, not anyone else's. You don't need to worry about something happening to Buc. Whatever happens, I will take care of you."

Thirty minutes into the prayer session I was still seeing and hearing words from God, as if He had opened up a floodgate of communication. I had never heard His voice so clearly.

Yvette turned to Paul, looking a little helpless. "What do I do now?" I had completely forgotten she was there. For the past thirty minutes, it had been just God and me, swept up in a whirlwind of words and pictures and heart-to-heart communication. I'm sure Yvette wondered if I would ever get to an end point.

Paul turned to Yvette. "You can ask God whether or not it's time to close." He turned back to the group. "This is a good thing to do whenever you're not sure if you should continue the prayer session or close. Just ask God, 'Lord, is it time to end?' and He'll tell you."

"I'm ready to be done," I piped up. I knew I had much more to pray about, but it was enough for one day. I was emotionally spent. But I also felt peaceful, just as Mary and Amanda had at the end of their sessions.

With the help of Straight 2 the Heart and the Holy Spirit, I had finally connected the dots; I saw where my problems and my negative thoughts—all of them—came from. The sadness, the depression, the melancholy, the control issues, the fear, the negativity—it all came from Satan. Some of it came from lies he had whispered to me even before my family broke up; and some of it came from my family's breakup. But the point was, these negative thoughts, negative traits, negative events, were all from him. All the negative parts of me were perversions of my true identity—or the person God had created me to be.

What a relief! What a relief it was to my depressed mind to know that *the depression did not stem from me.* What a relief to know that there *was* another mind available to me: a Spirit-led, Spirit-directed mind; a mind grounded in truth. As Romans says, "Letting your sinful nature [Satan] control your mind leads to death. But letting the Spirit control your mind leads to life and peace" (8:6, NLT).

All my life I had believed that my negativity was just who I was. But now I saw a bigger picture. I saw the great controversy being played out in my brain: Satan had sabotaged me with abandonment, rejection, and his countless lies; but, more important, Jesus had anticipated my abandonment and loneliness by suffering it, too, conquering it on the cross, and giving me the Holy Spirit to guide me into truth. So, the glorious truth was this: Jesus had already rewritten my story by suffering and dying on the cross—and now, as I continued to submit to His leadership, He could rewire my brain—He was changing me even now!

* * * * *

Eager for more of God's peace, I began praying on my own, applying what I had learned. Using my summary sheets from our group sessions, I began spending quiet mornings and evenings alone in prayer, seeking to further unfold the roots of my control issues. Suddenly, I couldn't get enough time on my knees. Often Buc walked in on me as I knelt by our couch or bed and commented, "Boy, Straight 2 the Heart really has you praying a lot."

I imagined he felt somewhat the way I used to when I walked in on Kyle praying. Now I knew how you could spend so much time on your knees: you spent as much time *talking* to God as you did *listening*.

During the day, if I identified a negative thought from Satan, such as, *I have to control my environment to protect myself,* or *I have to try harder and do more,* I stopped and prayed right then and there. Even better, when I shut up long enough to listen, I heard God speaking to me in new and healing ways. At first He didn't give me any action steps, or anything I could do to force something to happen, because He knew that my tendency to control, to try harder and do more, was one of my biggest ways of tuning Him out. Instead, He said, *"Lindsey, you can relax and stop trying to do it all in your own strength. For I know the plans I have for you, plans to prosper you and not to harm you; plans to give you hope and a future."*

Whenever the pain of my past came back to me, or when I was tempted to feel sorry for myself for not having my family around, I heard the voice of Jesus saying, *"I was a man of sorrows, well acquainted with grief. I was despised and rejected, and men esteemed me not. I know how you feel. I felt it too. But I also carried it to the cross—I nailed it there. I died once and for all, for you, but I am also a full service Savior, waiting to go with you again to any new pain, or any deeper pain, if it comes up. I am ready and willing to descend to your sorrows with you, to help you release and replace those sorrows."*

When that tendency came back to skip my time with God and to try and make plans in my own wisdom, God slowed me down and gently reminded me, *"Be still and know that I am God. Seek ye first the kingdom of God, and His righteousness. And all these things shall be added unto you."*

"But what things?" I prayed, still grappling with my career plans. One of my favorite Bible promises at this time was Psalm 37:4: "Take delight in the LORD, and he will give you the desires of your heart." But I was so confused. What were the desires of my heart? I didn't know. Or maybe I did, but they were too scary to admit.

For now, I decided to make prayer my top priority, using the model Paul had taught me. I would strive to hear God's voice and get intimate with His Word. In the end, wherever this praying took me—to graduate school, back to teaching, or maybe (did I dare consider it?) just home to have kids—I was committed to finishing this prayer journey I had started.

Chapter 23

Honoring My Losses

Summer 2012

Truth: "During the days of Jesus' life on earth, he offered up prayers and petitions with fervent cries and tears . . . and he was heard because of his reverent submission." —Hebrews 5:7

Honor and honesty have the same root word. We honor our losses as we are honest about them in prayer, surrendering them to our heavenly Father, just as Jesus did. —Paul Coneff

Some leaders at my church questioned the wisdom of this discipleship program: "Too revealing," they said. "It's too risky to share all our sins and secrets in front of one another." "We should never try to bring each other's sins to light." As training went on, I mourned these types of comments because they undercut the purpose of Straight 2 the Heart.

While it's true that sins, secrets, and ugly stories sometimes showed up in our prayer sessions, sharing those things was not the primary goal of the group; and sharing was always up to the person receiving prayer. As Paul told us, time and again, "We don't need to know the specific sin or behavior you are experiencing, unless you want to share. What we need in order to connect your heart to Jesus are those lies Satan has planted in you."

On the other hand, Paul told us that many people had never been "heard" in their lives. "Many people have never had the chance to share their story and have another human being just *listen* to them. So when you first offer to pray with people, one of the biggest gifts you can give them is listening to their story—*if* they want to share."

These words resonated with me. I compared my experience of sharing and praying in this group to my experiences of hiding in my Minnesota and Texas churches. It felt so much healthier to be honest with my church members rather than hide from them. For one, the burden of secrecy was lifted. For another, once they knew what was wrong with me, they could pray for me.

How, I wondered, could we truly and sincerely offer people "new life" if we weren't first willing to help them uproot the old one?

Straight 2 the Heart was the first Christian program I'd seen that honored the reality, both in preaching *and* in practice, that there is a *process* to being made "new in Christ." The program didn't promise instant change, it promised a process to help us take each layer of our bad fruits and roots to Christ. The program didn't just give us scriptures about becoming a new creation in Christ and leave us to figure out how to get there. It helped us *apply* those promises. The key was quality time, and repeated time, in prayer.

* * * * *

I eventually moved my personal prayer time from our open, airy breakfast nook into our dining room. This way, I could shut the door for privacy, and I could spread out my Bible, my prayer sheets, and Paul's seven-phase training manual. At this time, I was just beginning phase 1, "Honoring my Losses."

One of the activities in phase 1 was to articulate my losses in a few paragraphs. So one morning, I took out a clean sheet of paper and summarized my story, including my family's breakup; my depression and patterns of self-protection that followed; and more recently, my bitterness at Buc's happy family and anger at my own.

As I wrote, I had to wipe tears off the page. It was all becoming so clear now!

Yes, I had admitted that I envied Buc's happy family (a fruit); I had admitted that I had a problem with depression, and later with control (more fruits); but I had tried to disconnect that pain from the roots of my broken family. Before now, it hurt too much to examine the source.

But now I was facing those roots—and I had the secret weapon to defeat Satan's lies. Today, I knew a Savior who had suffered in every way I had, who had suffered the same losses I had, and who had words of comfort for me.

I thought back, as I often did, to the other part of Paul's presentation that first night he came to my church. The fruit/root principle, and Satan's lies, was what Paul called "the problem." But Paul had also presented "the solution." It was "The Hidden Half of the Gospel." It was another side to Christ's story that I hadn't heard before but that gave me hope like never before.

"Everywhere I go," Paul had said, "people tell me the gospel is three things: Jesus died for our sins, gave us forgiveness of our sins, and rose again." He paused to look around at the congregation. "I agree with that as far as it goes. The problem is that Jesus included more, and so did other Bible writers."

After another pause, Paul explained, "The Bible says Jesus was made in every way like us. Many, many scriptures include *suffering* in the definition of the gospel. Jesus Himself told His disciples He would have to *suffer*, die, and rise again, but *we* have not included *suffering* in our own definition of the gospel. We always just focus on the fact that Jesus died for our sins and rose again. And that's where we get our problem with ministering to people: we leave out the suffering. We leave out a Jesus who can identify with our pain.

"How would it make a difference to people if they saw a Savior who had gone through everything they had gone through? If we leave out the suffering of Jesus, then we don't have anything to offer people who are suffering from abandonment, betrayal, and abuse, or who are living on a cycle of sin-and-forgiveness. We can tell those people that God loves them and He forgives them, and that's great, but what do we tell people when they've been sinned *against*?"

The slide changed to a picture of a cross with a column on each side. One side listed the suffering of a woman who had been abused, and the other column listed the experiences Jesus had been through.

"How about offering this woman a Jesus who's been through the very same thing? How about a Jesus who was physically, mentally, and emotionally abused when He was stripped naked, beaten with whips, mocked and taunted? How about a Jesus who suffered *in every way* like her? Who can identify with her and understand her?"

Paul looked around the audience with a dead serious expression. "Would she be more willing to trust her Savior if she knew He understood how she felt?"

Wow. I was gripped, and so was everyone else.

And now, one month after sitting through that presentation and receiving prayer from my teammates—as I sat there writing out my losses and crying, crying, crying some more—I knew Paul was right. There was power in the story of Christ's suffering.

Knowing that Jesus had suffered like I had finally made it healthy and healing and OK to revisit my past.

Before then, whenever confronted with my past, or my losses, I didn't feel hope; I felt a gaping wound that couldn't be filled. Crying didn't bring relief, and grieving didn't bring relief. I felt as though I could cry forever and I would never expunge all the grief; rather, the crying only made it grow. But, finally, knowing Jesus' story of suffering made the difference between hope and hopelessness. The day that I "honored my losses" was the day my tears over my past turned to tears of joy. It was the day I discovered the difference between crying into a cavernous hole and crying in the arms of Jesus.

* * * * *

Shortly after our training began, Paul mentioned he was writing a book about his main message, "The Hidden Half of the Gospel." He said it with a grimace. The writing wasn't coming along so well; he was not a writer. But he *had* to get this book done. As a public speaker and prayer coach, he needed a resource to offer people who were eager for more—and having recently stepped down from pastoral ministry to incorporate Straight 2 the Heart, he needed the income.

At hearing this, I felt a glimmer of hope. *I want to help write this book!* I thought. But I didn't want to force God's hand, and I didn't want to force the writing dream if it wasn't God's plan, so I said nothing.

Later that summer, *Insight* magazine accepted an article I had submitted almost a year and a half before. Because the article chronicled my first suicide attempt, I kept it from most of my friends and family. But since Paul dealt with such subject matter all the time, I decided to give him a copy.

The day after I gave him the article, he called me, excited. "This was really great; this really flowed. I want my book to flow like this." Would I consider helping him write his book, he asked, which told the stories of other wounded, yet healing, adolescents-turned-adults?

"You don't have to ask twice," I said. My summer days morphed from writing my master's thesis to writing Paul's book. Now I wasn't only writing about myself (the only topic Buc said I ever wrote about), but I was also writing of real people who had suffered from abandonment, addiction, abuse, and betrayal, and received a new identity in Christ. It felt good, working to articulate the gospel through real life stories; in fact, it felt exactly like what I was meant to do.

By coincidence or divine appointment, I discovered a sale on composition notebooks at Target, and I picked up twenty without thinking twice. When I scooped up those notebooks, I didn't have specific plans for them. I just sensed I would need them for something. I stashed them in a desk drawer, vowing to return to them when I had some time.

And within a couple of months, when my other writing projects slowed down, I did have time. I pulled out one of those notebooks, and I started to write about all the roots my prayer sessions had brought up. I wrote about the loneliness I'd felt at moving to Texas, the sense of displacement in Buc's family, the anger I still felt at losing my own family, and my hurt at being unseen and unheard in my church. Above all, I wrote about how damaging it had been to keep quiet. I was surprised when I quickly filled one notebook, then two.

At the same time, my professor and thesis advisor, Jim Warren, leveled a writing challenge to our class: "Choose some audience that actually exists, and write your final paper to *them.*"

As I considered my now-bulging notebooks, I knew what I had to do. I had to start a blog. *That,* I told Jim, would be my real-world audience. But I knew the blog wouldn't stop at sharing my research on traditional versus self-publishing. Soon, I would share this personal writing I was doing. I felt it with each stroke of my pen: this was the next step in my healing—a way to reverse my toxic pattern of pretending things were OK when they weren't. It was a way to expose Satan's lies and break the silence that had cloaked, and deepened, my pain for too long.

Chapter 24

Answered Prayers, Big Decisions

Fall 2012

Truth: "For though we live in the world, we do not wage war as the world does. The weapons we fight with are not the weapons of the world. On the contrary, they have divine power to demolish strongholds. We demolish arguments and every pretension that sets itself up against the knowledge of God, and we take captive every thought to make it obedient to Christ."
—2 Corinthians 10:3–5

God is faithful. For so many years, I had felt empty space on the other end of my prayers. I had wondered where the Lord was and why He wasn't answering me. Now I knew that He had always been there, as Kyle had said; I just had to place myself in a position to hear Him. The Bible says to draw near to God, and He will draw near to us (James 4:8), and the closer I came to Him, the more I felt His presence. And the answers to prayer! Wow!

Once I started praying with Straight 2 the Heart, I felt answers coming every day. For the first few months, God didn't give me specific things to do; rather, He reminded me of His promises and exhorted me to keep relying on Him until He gave me specific steps. I want to make clear that one reason I was able to hear God's promises so clearly was that I had already committed a number of them to memory. God can certainly speak to us in various ways, but we greatly enhance our chances of hearing Him when we become familiar with His Word.

I prayed about my career choice for several months without hearing a clear answer. But I did consistently hear encouragement from God's Word, and I always found ways that Jesus could identify. For one, when I prayed about my sadness at leaving "home"—meaning Minnesota—I realized that Jesus had also left *His* home—heaven! The difference was, of course, that Jesus had left and lost much more than I had. For another thing, Jesus was tempted throughout His ministry to prove Himself, provide for Himself, and protect Himself. Finally, He was tempted to walk away from His mission instead of going through the pain. He was tempted to do the easy thing rather than the right thing.

During one of my earliest group sessions, when I prayed about my need to control, God brought the phrase "having kids" to my mind. But when my prayer partner asked the Lord if this was a blessing or barrier, I wasn't sure. I was still scared to have kids, and God didn't tell me at that time whether He wanted me to have kids or not. But before the session closed, He *did* bring to mind the blessing that "He wants my joy to be full." I felt comforted that whether or not I had kids, God would eventually fill my cup.

For the next few months, I struggled so very hard with my priorities—from how to spend my open summer days to how to spend the rest of my life. I wanted to do what God wanted me to do, but between all the busyness I had built into my life—mostly church activities, plus completing my master's degree—it was hard to sort out the very *best* things God had for me.

I was beginning to sense where God wanted to take me, and it wasn't graduate school, and it wasn't even being on all the church committees I was on. I was beginning to feel as though God had a different purpose for my life, and it was the one that resonated with my truest, deepest identity. It was the part of me that screamed *"Yes!"* but also the part of me that cowered back in fear. These were the things that came with no guarantees—the things that put me in a position of total vulnerability.

We started the prayer group in July, and it was mid-September before I had a breakthrough on my career/kids dilemma.

"I feel so flustered," I told the group one autumn night. "I have too much clutter in my life right now. I have so many options on the table that I feel I'm not getting anywhere at all. I think Satan is doing this to me; trying to confuse me. There are some things God wants me to do, but I'm scared to follow through with them. I'm so worried about what other people think that I say yes to every-thing, instead of saying no when I need to, and saying yes to the most important things."

Amanda was facilitating prayer that night, and she asked, as always, "How do you think Jesus can identify with you?"

This time as I listened for the Holy Spirit, I was impressed with the fact that Jesus knew all along what His purpose was—to suffer and die for humanity—and He carried it out, even though it was hard.

My God-given purpose might be hard to carry out, I thought, wilting a little. That wasn't what I wanted to hear. But God knew I was ready to hear it. Along with that, He told me, *"You have a lack of faith."* I knew it was my lack of faith keeping me from moving on. But again, the Holy Spirit told me I was getting closer to the goal; I just had to "keep praying," and I had to "let go," and I had to "receive more of Jesus' faith."

It wasn't easy to keep praying through this blind spot of faith. But I kept at it.

I kept praying, "Lord, what do You want me to do with my life? Where do I go at the end of December, after this master's degree is finished?"

And the next day, as I prayed at my desk, college brochures spread out before me, along with my empty notebooks, His answer came through loud and clear. *You know what to do,* God said.

As tears streamed down my cheeks, I realized I had known for months. It was only now that I had the faith to accept God's call.

* * * * *

"Honey, can you come home early from work?" I said to Buc over the phone. "We need to talk about our future."

An hour later, Buc walked through the door. "Is everything OK? You sounded upset on the phone."

"No, no, I'm not upset. I just have a lot to talk to you about. Let's drive to the state park and walk and talk."

When we started on our nature walk, words just started tumbling out of my mouth. "Honey, I looked at my life in the last few years—how I've been running around, keeping so busy, trying *so* hard—and I realized I lost sight of what I was doing. All throughout our eight years of marriage I've been so guarded about having kids. I've never forgotten the pain and the questions a divorce and a broken family bring to a child, and I've been terrified of passing that along to my own kids. So I've been fending off any possible desire for children by raising any and every objection I could think of. I told myself I didn't want children, or more family.

"I told myself I just had to 'try harder and do more,' and go it alone with no love and support. I made all my plans based on what I knew I could do, without help. And that's why I thought I 'wanted' a PhD and professorship. Because I knew, without a doubt, I could accomplish it.

"I didn't feel so confident about being a mom. But now . . . after going through all this prayer and healing . . ."

I looked up at Buc.

He looked right back at me. "You want to have babies?" he asked tenderly.

"Yes," I whispered, and that one word knocked the wind out of me.

Like a crashing wave this realization came. In all the years we'd been married, I had never been able to say it—to say that I wanted kids.

"Is it possible?" I marveled aloud to Buc. "Is it possible that all I've ever *really* wanted was to get back to having a family? To have *kids*? Is it possible that the one thing I've been so scared to embrace all these years is the one thing I've really just wanted to get back to?"

I was flabbergasted by the thought. As I talked about our future—a new future—I felt a weight lifting. Was it possible I was really letting go? Just letting the debris settle, and finally settling myself? The thought was comforting, even as it brought new fear.

I cringed and looked up at Buc. Would he approve of this change of plans?

"Honey? What do you think?" I shifted my eyes down. "What would you think if I decided to stay home and write, and maybe have some kids?" I held my breath.

But his touch was soft. "Honey, I think that sounds nice. I like the idea. I just have one question," he said, swinging my arm as we traipsed through the brush. "Why now? Why after all these years are you finally ready to have kids?"

I thought for a moment before answering, letting the happiness of the moment sink in.

"I think I finally understand something." I let my free arm drift across tree leaves, feeling like a little girl again. "The best parents—I mean the people who should be having kids—have them because they are already happy. They have them not to make themselves happy, but to share their happiness—to invite someone else into their special, intimate joy. They don't ask their kids to bring meaning to their lives, they ask to be able to share meaning with their kids."

"Well said," Buc beamed at me. "I think I've got a wise wife."

"Not that wise," I smiled back. "I'm just learning to take God's lead."

And that, I thought, *is something worth passing on to my kids!*

* * * * *

The day Buc and I wandered through the woods and decided to have kids, I didn't know I was also brushing up against poison ivy. Several days later found me scratching my skin, unable to think of anything but stopping the itch. Suddenly, I was like a rabid dog, ready to bite anyone who got too close.

"Don't touch me!" I screamed at Buc. The slightest tickle of fabric against my skin elicited a battle cry. So, too, did a phone call from a church member who needed a pianist on Sabbath. No one at church knew how I felt, so, of course, no one stopped their regular calls or emails about music or communications. But these contacts, like my husband's inadvertent brushing up against my rash, incensed me.

Stop! I wanted to roar. *Can't you see that I'm in pain?*

Over two weeks of maddening itching, I felt my poison ivy calling attention to another itch I had, another need that was going unmet: I wanted more people in my life. But not just in the way they had been in my life lately, in the form of ministry colleagues.

At that time, I was facilitating a Friday-night Bible study, a Tuesday-night prayer group, the church newsletter, and the church music committee—along with finishing my thesis and Paul's book—and I was worn out. Before the prayer training, I had barreled full force into too many activities, not only to do a good thing, but to try to fill my holes, and to try to prove myself good enough. This overextension of myself was, no doubt, a fruit of Satan's lies. But now I was suffering the consequences, and something had to change.

Lord, I'm so lonely! I prayed. *I see it now, Lord. I need fewer plans, more people.*

And I heard the promise: "God sets the lonely in families" (Psalm 68:6).

Oh yes, I need more family, I prayed, but this time I knew I was longing for more than just kids. I longed for genuine friends, and also for a mother figure. I wanted a woman (or maybe several) to adopt me, to take me under her wing like a surrogate daughter, to counsel me on career and kids and running a household.

And the Lord was very good. Almost immediately, He began to speak to me about this. But the full answer didn't come immediately, and it didn't come in the form of women knocking on my door. As He has told me so often since Straight 2 the Heart, God told me to look not at what others could do for me, but at what I could do for others. I realized I could keep wishing for friends and a mother figure in silence, or *I* could be the catalyst for change.

Suddenly, I had all these women from church on my mind, including women just down the street whom I rarely talked to, except in passing. Before then, I'd always worried that I'd be bothering them. But now that I'd spent more than a year in isolation, I knew better. We *needed* each other.

So I decided to reach out.

As head of music that year, I took a leap of faith and organized a church choir. Not because I needed one more thing to do, but because we had a lot of musical people in our congregation, and I knew that the small group atmosphere would bless these individuals. God answered on the first day I made the call for singers, even providing a choir director from within our midst! Tammy, who later became a good friend, had only visited our church up to this point; but ultimately she became a member because of the choir.

Beyond the choir, I started sending greeting cards to fellow church ladies just to say I appreciated them. I invited a couple of them out to lunch with me. I offered to pray with a depressed friend who had just moved back to the area. I prayed with a graduate classmate who always typed troubling things on Facebook. I started campaigning at church board meetings that we needed small groups—and Amanda and I started seeking for others to pray with.

For a while, no one responded. We made calls up front to form a new prayer group, to no avail. Eventually, we would find a number of women to pray with, but at first, I think people were scared of opening up. In the meantime, while we waited for a response, I decided to reach out to the woman I most wanted to connect with: Mom.

Chapter 25

Reaching Out

Winter 2013

"For we are God's handiwork, created in Christ Jesus to do good works, which God prepared in advance for us to do."
—Ephesians 2:10

Mom and I started talking on the phone every day that I commuted to graduate school. Our communication became more consistent than it had been in years. I told Mom about Straight 2 the Heart and some of the things I'd learned about myself. Then, I asked if I could pray with her.

During the first of many prayer sessions over the phone, Mom readily responded to a Jesus who had been manhandled and unjustly treated like a criminal, a Jesus who had been stripped of His clothes as well as His dignity. Mom couldn't see my tears over the phone, but I was seeing her in a new light. I didn't understand much about what caused bipolar disorder, but now I considered not only how *I* felt when Mom went to the hospital, but how *she* felt. I marveled at how Jesus had always understood.

During another prayer session, she brought up her father. He had died when she was five months old, and she said she always felt the void. "I guess because I never had that relationship with my father, it caused me to search for my heavenly Father," Mom explained. That night she connected with a Jesus who felt forsaken by His Father.

As Mom and I prayed together, I found more compassion for the mother who had abandoned me (but never stopped loving me) because I saw how many struggles we had in common. I saw a child who had been abandoned by a parent when she was only five months old. I saw a girl who had learned to doubt herself at a young age, because her mother didn't have time or sufficient attention to give. I saw a teenager who had looked to the wrong guys for the love and affirmation she didn't find at home. I saw a fresh-faced bride so young and so unready to marry—but who *had* married, nonetheless, because she was desperate to find a safe place to call home. Finally, I saw an adult woman who had sacrificed herself, and her voice, to her husband, her in-laws, and her new surroundings—a woman who had left behind too many parts of herself to be whole. When she told me during one of our talks that she felt like a "fraction of a person" in her first marriage, I understood, because that's how I had felt for so many years.

These conversations helped me see how much I missed her, and how much of a loss I felt for not having her close in my adult life. I began to pray that, somehow, we could regain some of the ground we had lost; that together, we could grow into whole and healthy women. I knew our relationship was not all better yet, but I trusted God to move us to the next level when the time was right.

* * * * *

For me, a big part of becoming "whole and healthy" was writing. After I started writing in my bargain notebooks, which I later dubbed my "Writing to My Roots" notebooks, I felt my true identity emerging, especially because a goal of Straight 2 the Heart is to help people claim their true identities in Christ. My writing became the vehicle through which that identity manifested itself. Suddenly my words overflowed, almost as if I couldn't control where and when, and to whom, I might expose myself.

Another Christmas season came and went, and with the New Year came another new start. I had completed our prayer and discipleship training, and I had completed my master's degree. As of now, my full-time job was . . . well, to share the healing I'd found, and to begin trying for a baby.

In January 2013, I began my blog, *Writing to My Roots,* and at Paul Coneff's request, Amanda and I helped start another prayer group in a neighboring church; we prayed with a small group of women and trained them to do the same. With both my blog and the prayer training, I shared my story, gaining confidence every time my readers or listeners responded positively, and their feedback was all positive. Meanwhile, Amanda and I continued seeking for women in our own congregation to pray with.

Finally, after several months, we found two women in our congregation who responded to our call.

* * * * *

Christina and Ashley were both close to us in age, and both new to our congregation. Both had recently returned to church after rebellious teens and twenties, which included three divorces and four children between the two of them. It was no surprise that the two of them became fast friends. As Paul often reminded us during training, "We tend to trust people we can identify with. That's why Jesus chose to identify with us in every way."

Amanda made their acquaintance first because I was at this time still too tied up at the piano and with other church roles to meet them during church hours. (This underscored for me all over again how important it was to have small groups outside of church settings: sometimes church is simply too busy to get to know people.)

In her quiet and sincere way, Amanda sat down with Ashley and Christina and shared her testimony from Straight 2 the Heart. She was planting seeds to see if they were ripe fruit for similar healing . . . and they were!

Christina confided that she was still dealing with shame and guilt for two failed marriages, and for having three children with three different men. She said she loved our church but worried that most of our members would judge her if she shared her past.

"I've been praying for godly friends like you and Lindsey who could support me and help me as I try to do what's right," she confessed.

"Me too," Ashley agreed. "I'm in, as long as Christina is."

When Amanda and I talked later, Amanda said to me, "We need to nurture them."

"Like we were nurtured," I agreed.

* * * * *

What happened next was another humbling period of healing and growth, not only for Ashley and Christina, but also, again, for me. For four months, we met on Tuesday nights at Christina's house, and Amanda and I alternated facilitating prayer. One week one of us prayed with Ashley, the next week, the other prayed with Christina. The four of us grew close over those months.

Paul had taught us it was best to work as partners, to make disciples of people in pairs, because Jesus had sent out His disciples two by two. Now following that precedent, we saw the wisdom in the two-by-two method. On some nights, either Amanda or I was busy, but the other one could still facilitate. On other nights, either Ashley or Christina was tempted to cancel from a rough day. That was when the other one called and encouraged, "This is when you need prayer the most!"

I should mention that in our original prayer group nearly a year before, I had not gone through the entire seven-phase process. Much of that time was focused on training; plus, both Amanda and I found that the first three phases, centered on our known and unknown losses, brought up so many roots that it was all we could do to pray through *those*!

Now, praying with our two new friends, we entered phase four and beyond, and these phases moved all of us into thinking about others: we prayed about how our patterns of self-protection had hurt others; we prayed about our inherited generational patterns; we prayed for Christ's supernatural spirit of forgiveness; and finally, we prayed that Christ would help us honor our callings in ministry.

I can't express how much I appreciated this design of praying through our losses first, and leaving relationships and forgiveness for later. As I thought about the order of the phases, I realized that Paul Coneff with Straight 2 the Heart followed the same wisdom that Stephen Covey followed with his Seven Habits. In both programs, the first three phases, or habits, focus on self; the remaining steps move into our relationships. And it makes sense. It is for the same reason that flight attendants tell parents, "Don't try to help your children put on *their* mask until you have secured *yours.*"

By the time I became a prayer facilitator for my new friends, I certainly wasn't done with my own healing. I definitely had some roots left in the relationship department—some anger and bitterness and unclaimed responsibility—but I *was* trying. I was trying to deal with unresolved relationship problems as they came up in my personal prayer times, and as they came up in my daily life.

The three relationships that I decided needed the most repair were with Margie, Dad, and Mom. And that's the order in which I dealt with them. I had the least history with Margie, so it was easiest to deal with her first.

Right before Christmas, I had again felt bitterness surface. It was the same story as in previous years: I missed my own family, and I resented the closeness I saw in the Gendkes. Because Margie was the mastermind behind the grand Christmas ceremony, she unfairly got my blame. I had never told her how I felt—how her elaborate Christmas ceremonies saddened me, or how out of place I still felt in her family—but I had harbored these feelings for years. So that Christmas, at the tail end of Paul Coneff's training, I decided to write her a letter of apology. It was really more for my benefit than hers because I knew it was important for me to learn to voice my feelings in this family. Indeed, it probably came as a surprise, as we had always had a friendly relationship. But after the letter, the next time she saw me, Margie gave me a big hug and said, "You are part of this family too; and we love you! Don't ever feel like you're not important to us." And that was all she needed to say.

I felt loved in that moment, and I began to believe that I really could fit into Buc's family. Christmases after that got easier, and Margie and I grew closer. I confided in her my new wish for a baby, and she hugged me and prayed for me. I praised God for having such a godly mother figure close by; and I prayed that soon I would have her help in raising a child of my own.

Several months after that, while completing phase 3 with Ashley and Christina (my second time through phase 3), suddenly Dad was on my mind. Part of phase 3 asked me to examine whom I'd hurt by my patterns of protection, and that's what made me realize Dad deserved an apology as well.

I had treated him badly after Mom left, and I had never made it right. Blinded to Dad's feelings by my own, I had not considered the depth of his pain when his wife, his son, and his daughter all left him within a period of two years.

Only now did I start to wonder how he really felt. His wife hadleft him, his son went off to college, and then his teenage daughter left—and all because he was trying to offer help in the only ways he knew how.

I felt terrible now that we had all left Dad around the same time, and I wanted to acknowledge my disrespectful behavior toward him during that period. So I wrote him a letter of apology. The next time we talked on the phone, all dear Dad said about the letter was: "I don't remember us not getting along. It was a nice letter, but it wasn't necessary."

I was stunned. How could he not remember those knockdown, drag-out fights I described in my journals? How could he forget this stuff so easily?

"Dad is so out of touch," I told Buc, as I had told him many times throughout our marriage. This phone call seemed like one more demonstration of that fact.

"You should give him more credit," Buc told me, yet again. "Just because you don't hear him talk about that emotional stuff doesn't mean he's not aware of it." Buc went on to tell me about a private conversation he'd had with Dad about the family breakup during our first visit to Minnesota. "Your dad told me that he felt trapped; he wasn't sure which way to go. He wanted to keep the family together, but your mom would not leave Ray, and he didn't know how to react to that. He said he was trying to keep the family together, but no matter what he did, things just didn't work out. He also said he felt a lot of remorse about the family breaking up and what it would do to the kids."

I pondered Buc's words, and I decided to try to understand Dad better. I wanted to understand why he'd had such trouble expressing his feelings when I was a teenager, and why he still avoided talking about the "deep stuff" these days.

In phase 4 of Paul's training, "Generational Patterns," I formed a hunch that Dad's emotional distance came from his own parents. I remembered that neither Dad nor most of his siblings had cried at my grandpa's funeral. By contrast, when Margie's mother died, I'd watched her wail for fifteen minutes over the body before it was taken away.

Over a series of conversations with Dad, I pried into this subject, along with his relationship with Mom. "Dad, do you think your parents ever played favorites with you kids?"

With barely a delay, he answered (in the same tone he might field, "How do you take your coffee?"), "Nope. They never told *any* of us they loved us."

Laughter escaped both our lips.

"How sad!"

"Yep, I never saw my parents kiss, and I never heard them tell each other they loved each other."

"Well, Grandma tells me she loves *me* when I call," I said.

"That's because Juanita and I started telling her that."

Dad told me, with disbelief, that Juanita talked to her kids, her parents, *and* her favorite brother *every single day.* Clearly, Juanita's family structure had upset Dad's ideas about family—just like Buc's family structure had challenged mine. *Huh,* I thought. *Dad and I actually have something in common!*

Indeed, after Juanita entered the picture, Dad had started calling me on a regular basis—usually once a week or so. And now he gave me not just a hug at the airport but a kiss on the cheek too.

Give him more credit, Buc's voice echoed in my mind.

Dad and Juanita read love and marriage books together, his favorite being *Men Are From Mars, Women Are From Venus.* In the months after he read it, he referenced it frequently. And during our talks about family, he repeated his favorite nuggets of wisdom.

"Men want to go to their caves sometimes."

"Women just need to be told they're loved. They need hugs."

"The best thing parents can do for their kids is to show affection to one another."

"It's just amazing how men and women are so *different!*"

Most often Dad's statements on marriage were sweeping and general, but once in a while he slipped in a sentence such as, "I should have been doing these things with your mom."

I thought about those sentences, and how he actually *was* doing those things with Juanita. So maybe he hadn't dug up all his negative "roots," and maybe he'd missed some of the signs with me, but these days, he *was* making an effort. When I saw him kiss Juanita in the mornings, or bring her coffee as she applied her makeup—and I paired it with a sentence such as, "I didn't hug Su enough," I knew he had regrets. He didn't have to say it.

I gave Dad his credit.

* * * * *

Meanwhile, because I kept my heart humble and teachable, admitting to our four-person group that I still needed prayer as much as anyone, God blessed my broken efforts. In our new group, God used *everyone's* brokenness—Ashley's, Christina's, Amanda's, and mine—to help us help one another. I am certain that everyone's healing and faith was multiplied simply because we got to walk through the program together—because we got to see God working not only in our own lives but also in each other's lives.

Just as Amanda and I had done almost a year earlier, Ashley and Christina began the healing process by honoring their losses and then connecting their stories with Jesus' story.

When our Tuesday-night meetings began, Ashley had been taking Bible studies from her mother-in-law for almost a year, but she told us there were still many barriers in her heart keeping her from surrendering to God. The main barrier was anger: anger at a father who had abused her as a young child, and anger at a stepfather who kept her in a cockroach-infested drug house. Growing up surrounded by booze and smoke, she took this path too. She met her husband, Kevin, when she was a teenager, and the two of them ended up partying together; getting pregnant with their daughter, Katelynn; and finally getting married. In Ashley's current life, often her anger boiled over to Kevin and Katelynn, she told us, and she wanted that to stop.

As we prayed week after week, Ashley was able to identify with Jesus because He had been mistreated, abused, and tempted to get angry at His tormentors. Along with acknowledging Ashley's losses, we also prayed that when her anger came, she could pause and let Jesus fight for her. Within a few weeks, she reported the battle getting easier.

As Ashley let Jesus deal with her anger, she was able to let Him deal with her guilt at her past lifestyle too. One memorable night she confessed that she felt like too bad of a sinner to be accepted by God. When we cracked open Luke 15 and the parable of the lost sheep, tears sprang to her eyes. "That lost sheep is me," she exclaimed. Yes, we said, God rejoiced more for her than for His sheep that had never strayed!

At the end of four months and seven phases, Ashley was able to speak of her deceased father without anger because she acknowledged that he had probably been abused too, and he didn't know how else to raise her. She even met up with her step-siblings and, for the first time, was able to enjoy herself in their presence. During phase 6 (identifying Christ's calling in her life), she heartily concluded that God was calling her to minister to children. "This phase came right in time," she said, "because I've been invited to help with the Adventurer Club, and I was feeling inadequate." Phases 6 and 7 helped her pray through the barriers that threatened to keep her from her God-given calling.

The key issues that emerged for Christina were guilt over her children's three fathers, especially the one who had disowned his son, and loneliness at being single. "I just want to rush into another relationship because it's so hard doing this motherhood thing alone; plus, it gets so lonely!" she lamented. "But I don't want to run ahead of God either. You see how that's worked out for me in the past!"

For four months these themes recurred. Christina's abandonment by her father had led her into a succession of bad relationships. These, in turn, had left her with three fatherless kids and tons of guilt—yet her loneliness and desire for relationship remained. After grappling with this pain for several sessions, and then taking responsibility for how her own behavior had worsened her circumstances, she heard God saying, *"I am the man you need; focus on Me."* And she gained peace.

At one of our meetings, about two months in, Christina sat down positively glowing. "You guys," she effervesced. "I'm telling you, I was having my time with God in the morning, and these words just started coming to me! See?" She held up a sheet of paper, filled from top to bottom with her swirly script. "But these were not my words! God was talking to me, you guys! I have never heard Him so clearly as I am hearing Him now!"

By the end of the four months, Christina's major victory was forgiving the father of her "abandoned" child. "I don't feel angry at him anymore," she said. To his surprise, she even wrote him a letter of forgiveness. She learned to concentrate on what *she* could do as a mother, not on what the fathers of her children were or were not doing. As to claiming her true calling? "I feel like *my* mission field is ministering to my own family," she said. And I saw that in her. Christina had the gift of hospitality that not many possess, frequently inviting friends and family to her warm and welcoming house for Sabbath lunches or game nights. That, indeed, was effective outreach!

"I'm going to miss these nights together," Ashley and Christina said on our last night. Amanda and I felt the same way. We had learned that nothing bonds friends like heartfelt, corporate prayer. Through listening to and praying for one another, we had borne each other's burdens and derived encouragement. Hearing one another's struggles and victories through Jesus had heartened us, and kept us accountable to continue praying. It was with mixed emotions that we ended our prayer group, but we all knew God was calling us in other directions.

Christina and Ashley began helping with our church's children's ministries. Amanda got involved with vespers, became a Sabbath School superintendent, and started participating in prison ministry. And me?

I was on the brink of another new start. I was pregnant! Knowing I needed to conserve my energy, I prayed for God to show me the most important things. And, of course, when we ask God where He wants to fix us, He always answers!

Chapter 26

The Fruit of Forgiveness

Spring, Summer 2013

Truth: " 'I am the vine; you are the branches. If you remain in me and I in you, you will bear much fruit; apart from me you can do nothing.' " — *John 15:5*

"Forgiveness is so important that Jesus took time out from dying to do it" (see Luke 23:34; Reggie McNeal, page 173 in A Work of Heart, *Jossey-Bass, 2000).*

Again and again in prayer groups I've facilitated (as of this writing, three groups), I end up identifying with the women I am praying with and learning things about my own healing journey. Not surprisingly, as I walked through the seven phases with Ashley, Christina, and Amanda, I related to their struggles of forgiving those who had hurt them. And this gave me a good idea where God wanted to take me next.

Paul Coneff has something he calls the "fruit test," based on Galatians 5. When we think of a person, event, or memory that once brought pain—let's call these our "triggers"—we can ask a question to see whether we are healed or not: What kind of fruit springs into our hearts and minds? If our "triggers" bring love, joy, peace, patience, and the other fruits of the Spirit, then we can know we are healed. If, on the other hand, those triggers bring us bitterness, anger, hurt, or tears, then we know we have some more healing to do.

Let me celebrate for a moment what *didn't* bring me bitterness anymore. It didn't bring bitterness to think about my family's breakup. It didn't bring anger or hatred to think about Mom's affair or my parents' divorce. And let's talk about forgiveness. I'm not sure when it happened exactly—maybe while I was praying on the phone with Mom?—but I knew in my heart that I had forgiven her for her affair and for leaving our family. Once I heard her side of the story, it felt almost natural for me to forgive those things because I could identify with the pain that had led her to them. In fact, God had brought me into a place where I could talk about my family's split, in prayer trainings and on my blog, with peace. It didn't hurt much to tell *that* story—the old story that was closed and done with.

What *did* hurt, what *did* bring me anger and bitterness, were the *results,* or the *consequences,* of some of my parents', especially Mom's, decisions. Fortunately, we can sin and receive forgiveness from God and from others—and we can have assurance of a brand-new, sinless life in heaven one day. Unfortunately, this wonderful hope doesn't mean that we won't still suffer consequences for our sins while on this earth. And there were consequences that my family still suffered because of the same sins God had thrown into the depths of the ocean. These consequences were my triggers.

Every time I visited Minnesota, or thought of visiting Minnesota, I got a little angry. My parents lived more than two hours apart, and this meant travel was always clunky, and time with each parent always shortened. Furthermore, with this divided setup, I rarely had time to visit old friends.

Every time I saw a mother and an adult daughter hanging out together, just the two of them, I got a little angry. Because Mom had started a new family fifteen years earlier, with another young child to raise (although I loved Caleb dearly), I had virtually lost fifteen years—and crucial years—of mothering. She had missed so many big things: advising me on my first period, giving me a sex talk, and helping me choose a husband. For that matter, after I was out of her house, we missed lots of little things, "normal" mother-daughter things, such as going shopping, taking road trips, or going out to dinner, just the two of us. Buc defined this loss by saying I had a "mommy complex"—I wanted my mom to be there for me in ways that she simply could not be, living so far away and being married to a man who was not my dad. It's not that she didn't want to be there for me, it's just that these were our unfortunate consequences.

I didn't make these feelings known to Mom, unless they seeped through without my notice. No, I tried to contain them, so I would not add more pain to what she already carried. I tried to assure Mom that I had forgiven her for leaving our family. And I had, of course. But maybe she sensed that I was still angry about our other losses.

* * * * *

"How can I heal from this, Lord?" I prayed on my own. "Why does this pain go on—why do these triggers still hurt so much? Is there a way to stop them?"

"Forgive her, for she knows not what she did," God said (see Luke 23:34).

This was a verse we had talked about often in prayer group. Just like Jesus, who prayed this amazing prayer on the cross, we should forgive others because they don't know in full what they are doing when they sin against us. When Mom had her affair, and when she left, she didn't know all the negative fruit that would result. She didn't know that her children would become emotionally and physically distant; that I would become suicidal; that Kyle would lose respect for her; that our visits (when we finally reconciled) would become logistical nightmares; or that she would lose so much precious time with her kids.

Of course, I needed to forgive Mom for these secondary losses. But it was hard. It was impossible . . . without Jesus.

Straight 2 the Heart to the rescue, again!

Just like so many Christian concepts that Paul Coneff had "made over" in my brain, he gave me a new understanding of forgiveness.

He taught that instead of forgiveness being something I could *do*, it was a gift I could *receive* from Jesus (phase 5). Forgiveness was not natural; it was supernatural. The only things I could do were to ask God for His supernatural gift of forgiveness, and then pray through any barriers keeping me from receiving that gift.

So, I prayed: "Dear Jesus, are there any negative beliefs in my heart keeping me from receiving Your Spirit of forgiveness for Mom, for the things she did not know she was doing to me, and for the pain she did not know she was causing me?"

As I had often done in the past year, I "facilitated" several prayer sessions for myself, writing out the blessings and barriers and roots the Holy Spirit brought to me. And God was so good, so thorough in the answers He gave!

At first, the barrier of anger came up. I was angry at Mom for being passive, for being too quiet when she should have spoken up, because I knew I had inherited this trait from her. And I was angry at her for letting her past dictate her future. I was angry that she had become a victim of circumstances, letting herself get pulled into more than one unwise relationship, and putting her vocational dreams on hold because she was still dealing with the fallout of those decisions.

But as I continued to pray, God revealed that my "anger" at Mom was really fear—fear that my story would end up like hers, full of unspoken thoughts, unfulfilled needs, and unclaimed dreams.

I thought of how Mom was still so guarded about her pain, and I knew that it was the "lie of silence" that had sabotaged her. And, to my surprise, I realized that this "lie of silence," this lie that we couldn't speak up or have needs, was the same root that had led to my parents' bad marriage and our ensuing family problems. What do I mean?

If Mom and Dad had been honest about what each one needed before their marriage, they would not have "sacrificed" their happiness for the other; they would not have married. As it was, Mom chose Dad because he was the "safe" man (not necessarily the right one), and Dad did the "nice" thing by agreeing to marry Mom and ignoring his gut feeling (that the marriage wasn't necessarily the right thing).

Later, when Mom was diagnosed with bipolar disorder, the "lie of silence" sprouted again. The diagnosis was so shameful, so insulting, that Mom denied it, taking meds only to get doctors off her back, and then, always going off her meds later, to repeat the cycle over and over again. She never warned anyone she was going off her meds; she tried to take care of her problems on her own, doing what made the most sense to *her*. But by that time, problems were too far out of hand, past the point of reasoning, and she ended up at the hospital. I had heard no productive dialogue about a better solution; I'd just seen impulsive actions when tensions rose, and then crisis. I had seen, over and over again, problems escalate from zero to sixty. Through sudden behaviors and words, elephants would pop up that I wasn't even aware of, and then Mom would suddenly be whisked off to the hospital. Surely there was a better way.

Mom has wondered aloud many times since we started talking about these things what would have happened if Dad, or her siblings, or the doctor that initially diagnosed her, had paused to investigate why she didn't seem like herself back in the year of the diagnosis—the same year that I, the unhappy, melancholy baby, was born. That year saw her caring for two young children mostly alone, without family nearby, and while her only surviving parent was diagnosed with Alzheimer's and put into a nursing home.

What if the treatment she'd received wasn't a bottle of pills, or *only* a bottle of pills, but a support system, some babysitters, several nights of uninterrupted sleep, and a prayer group? What if someone had simply offered to pray with her through her roots, her losses?

It's still such a confusing issue. I don't have all the answers, and I'm not saying Mom's diagnosis either is or is not correct. But I know one thing: Satan was able to do a lot of damage to Mom, Mom's family, Dad, and us kids, because we simply never tackled the "bipolar thing" head on. Something was definitely going on with Mom when she received the diagnosis—a lot of things—and it's simply a tragedy that neither Mom, nor Dad, nor anyone else could talk honestly about those things before they grew into big, fat, killer elephants.

At the point when I was praying for forgiveness, Mom was often still too timid to voice her concerns, especially when they might offend someone else (no matter if that someone else had hurt her). Seeing how she still suffered for her silence was what most angered me, what made me most afraid, and what kept me from forgiving her.

But when I asked the Lord for His blessings, He gave me many. I heard the words: *"Mom's life is not a blueprint for mine; and her track record of handling things alone and in silence does not have to be **my** track record."*

Further, as I prayed, I felt convicted to share these things with Mom. This would undoubtedly mean some hard conversations; but for this fear, God assured me I could pray about how to be honest with her, and I could also write about it. Healing was coming, and forgiveness was coming, as long as I didn't close up—and as long as I didn't buy into the lie of silence.

No matter how our conversations went, it was comforting to know that my story was my own. I had a lot of life ahead of me, and I had the choice and the ability, with Jesus' help, to write my own ending.

Chapter 27

All Things New

Fall 2013

Truth: "The thief comes only to steal and kill and destroy; I have come that they may have life, and have it to the full."
—John 10:10

I kicked one foot out of our satin sheets and threw off our royal purple comforter. "*Oooh*, I'm burning up. I'm hungry, babe," I added, nuzzling against Buc's warm back. This was how a lot of our Saturday mornings started lately.

Buc rolled over. "You're always hungry in the mornings."

"No," I corrected, rubbing my belly. "*Our baby* is always hungry in the mornings!"

"Is that a hint?" he grinned, placing his hands over mine. Buc threw off the covers and headed for the kitchen. I lounged for several more moments, counting my blessings, soaking in the Sabbath. God had commanded me to rest on this day, and I was finally grateful He had. I appreciated the fourth commandment even more, thinking of the new life that was soon to join our family. With Buc working all week, the Sabbath had become our best day—a time to connect with God, and a time to reconnect with each other. Soon, it would become a day when Buc could spend extra time with our son. Seeing Buc play with our child was one of the things I anticipated the most. I knew, from watching him play with our nieces and nephew, that he would be a great dad.

I, on the other hand, felt really awkward around kids, but I didn't worry about that anymore. I figured God would lead me through this adventure, as He had led through every other challenge.

I slipped on my favorite maternity dress and padded through our hallway, pausing to imagine our many rooms filled with laughter. We had a large house, and it was time to fill it up—for good.

I stopped when I came to the living room, breathing prayers of thanks for how the Lord was already hard at work filling up my home, and filling up my life, with exactly what I'd asked for: friends, and mother figures, to support me. My current prayer group met on Friday nights here, in this very room.

From our very first weekend we had connected. Ten women—ten women!—from my local congregation, some old friends, and some new, had sprawled in this living room, on my couch, on my floor, spilling their stories as though we'd been close friends forever.

And one more woman. Mom. *My* mom. I had invited Mom to be part of our women's weekend, the weekend that kicked off our three-month group. And she had come! She had come to Texas, for the first time all by herself, to pray with me and to spend time with me, as I navigated my first pregnancy, and got this women's group off the ground.

That weekend, after all the other women had received prayer, Mom took her turn. We broke for Sabbath lunch, and she was the only one left who hadn't shared (again putting others before herself).

But as we put out the buffet of sandwiches, chips, and goodies, Mom spoke up. "I guess it's time to tell my story," she said, dishing up her plate.

We sat down around the dining table that had seen so many of my tears and prayers, and Mom began the long task of telling.

By the time lunch was over, Mom was still talking, and there was only time left for a short prayer. But that was OK. Paul's words came back to me, "Many people have never been heard in their lives. One of the greatest gifts you can give these people is to simply listen to them." I was so proud of Mom for her courage.

Amanda led Mom through a short prayer, and then she asked me and one other woman to close the session by praying over her. I moved to sit by Mom on the couch. We embraced, and with tears in our eyes, I prayed.

"Dear Lord, thank You for my mom. I thank You for her courage to tell her story today to all these women, but I thank You that You already know all the details. Thank You for the beautiful person Mom is; and thank You that even though the enemy has attacked her, she is still Your child, and still my mom. I ask that You assure Mom of Your acceptance of her—help her see herself through Your eyes, and help her feel the forgiveness that You've already given her, and that I've already given her.

"And forgive me, Lord, if I haven't been the daughter that You want me to be. Help me, Lord, to honor my mother. Thank You for Your healing in both our lives; thank You that You will continue to heal us and bring us closer together. In Jesus' name, amen."

Mom squeezed me hard and for several long moments didn't let me go. I got a little embarrassed because she was making such a show of affection, and neither of us could control our tears. But then the Lord reminded me: *"This is what you've waited for. Your Mom is here. Your Mom is holding on, and this time she won't let you go. She loves you. And don't forget it."*

I was jolted from my memories of that prayer weekend by two furry tails swishing against my ankles. "Hi Bill. Hi Ted!" I greeted our new lab mix puppies. "Are you having an excellent morning so far?" This was *Buc's* way of filling up our house.

The little fur balls were roadside rescues from Brady. In a few months when baby Sam came along—we had decided to name him after our much-loved matchmaker, Samantha—the "boys" would roll right off the tongue: Sam, Bill, and Ted. I still couldn't believe how fast life was changing!

"Can you believe it was only one year ago that we took that walk in the woods, honey?" I asked Buc, sitting down to a breakfast of whole-wheat pancakes.

Buc scooped me up in his arms. "The most expensive walk of my life!" My particular case of poison ivy had ended up costing us two doctor visits, two steroid prescriptions, and a slew of topical creams. Now, there were monthly obstetrician visits, professional maternity clothes for my new job as adjunct English professor at Southwestern Adventist University, and baby supplies to pay for . . . which would soon transition to infant supplies, toddler needs, kid stuff, school bills. Basically, we would be paying for that walk for the rest of our lives! But even that didn't worry me. Buc had been promoted in his company, had a comfortable pocket of investments and a solid retirement plan.

"Now here we are with our very own little peanut on the way!" I turned and kissed my husband.

"Ready or not!" he added.

* * * * *

When we arrived at church, I stopped in front of the sanctuary but didn't go in. I lingered in the halls instead, because, right then it was more important for me to mingle with the people. In preparation for baby Sam, I had cut myself loose from the piano rotation. Buc was cutting back, too, but he would continue teaching the new Sabbath School class we'd started for young adults such as Christina and Ashley.

As I walked the halls, poking my head into the children's classrooms and greeting the teachers, one of them commented on my belly: "This will be a wonderful change!"

"Yes," I agreed. "It's already been a wonderful change."

"There's that new mommy!" my sister-in-law and the Kindergarten teacher, Deborah, squealed, meeting me halfway down the hall. I laughed as she rubbed my belly. "Hey, Sam! How ya' doin'? Aunt Deb can't wait to meet you!" She turned her attention from my belly to my face.

"Hey, Linds! How are *you* feeling?"

"Great!" I beamed. Aside from a little backache, I *did* feel great. Already, I felt a new realm of belonging opening up. Motherhood all by itself was opening doors to connect to more and more women, including Deborah, Margie, and Joanna.

Over my years of being a Gendke, I had inserted my voice more into family conversations, but not until I became pregnant did I feel I could really join the conversation. No matter who you are, or how bonded you are with your family, a baby provides a fresh start, a clean slate, for people to grab on to. And we had all grabbed on. With Sam growing in my womb, my in-laws had opened their arms and hearts to me in ways they hadn't before (or maybe I just hadn't noticed), and I had opened my heart to them.

Deborah had orchestrated a beautiful baby shower and lovingly made the only wall decorations that hung in Sam's room. Margie had been dropping off gifts for Sam as early as two months into my pregnancy—picture frames, Christmas ornaments, a night-light. And as my due date approached, Joanna dropped off baby clothes, called to ask if there was anything I needed from Target, and offered to babysit. Never had I felt so loved by this family, or so glad to be a part of it.

But that was how life felt, lately: new doors were opening all around me, and not just for me. Christina and her oldest son had been baptized a month earlier, and that day Ashley and Kevin were getting baptized.

I stepped into the sanctuary and paused, just looking around at all my friends, both old and new: Tammy, Susan, Eugenia, and Devon were new; and Julie, Linda, Mary, and Amanda were old friends I was getting to know better. Like Ashley and Christina, these women thought I was ministering to them; they didn't know they were also ministering to me. They didn't know how much being known and heard by them had changed the climate of church for me. Now every week I looked forward to church, because of my friends. I take that back. These women had become more than that; they had become my family.

I watched from a pew halfway up the aisle as Ashley and Kevin took their places in the baptismal tank. Ashley stepped forward and leaned into the microphone. "It's been a long journey, and we walked away, far away," she said. "But God never gave up. He was always knocking on the doors of our hearts. It wasn't God who walked away; He was always there. I'm so glad He never gave up on me."

"Amen," I said out loud, fumbling for tissue. *Thank You, Lord,* I prayed silently, because I knew what Ashley meant. I knew about that long journey to new life she had taken. But I wondered how many others did.

I wondered how many people here knew her story: the story of a life reborn, a past rewritten. I wished she would share the whole thing, so they would really know what it is to be buried with Christ and rise to new life. I wished there were time in the program for this. What better sermon could be preached? There were teens, young adults, and adults of all ages there who didn't understand what it meant to be "born again," and who were desperate to know, but perhaps didn't know how desperate they were. They wouldn't realize it until their homes, their families, their lives blew up one day and they were left without a clue as to how faith, or prayer, or Jesus could heal their wounds.

But I sat back and relaxed, knowing Ashley would tell. Maybe this particular crowd wasn't her audience, but I knew God would show her who was. I knew this because I had learned that when Jesus transforms you, you can't help sharing. He finds a way to reach straight into your heart, and then He gives you the words to share what He's done.

Epilogue

L ooking back, I see two rules that guided my survival after my family's crisis:

1. When you are in the middle of a shameful situation, keep quiet.
2. When that situation gets too hard to take, leave.

Now I recognize that these "coping mechanisms" were tools of the enemy to drive us further from help; and the only way I was going to find true healing was to be honest. But it took lots of prayer and writing and talking to trusted friends to make the connection. After I completed my Straight 2 the Heart training, I started blogging to further my healing, and I kept finding the theme of honesty and openness coming up. I realized I was trying to find an audience to talk about these things I'd bottled for more than a decade; without doing so, I couldn't finish healing.

Why is honesty so powerful? I believe it is because it is a "great controversy" issue. Let me explain.

Late in this manuscript's development, I was reading *The Great Controversy* for the first time. I had never read it before because, frankly, the story it told—the history of Satan's warfare on Christianity—seemed too far removed from my problems. But at age thirty, as an adult who had largely healed from depression and gained some perspective on suffering at large, I had a new capacity to receive Bible truth and the Spirit of Prophecy. I was able to turn my attention from myself (and from memoirs and self-help books) to this massive book of countries and peoples and religions and history.

But about halfway through the reading, I realized something. Ellen White's epic book about the controversy between Christ and Satan told the same story my manuscript did, just on a larger scale. The theme of my story, I realized then, was also Satan's warfare on Christianity, but warfare at the level of the family unit, and also at the level of the mind. Using primarily lies of silence (*I can never tell, I have to be "nice," I can't speak up or have needs*), Satan, that great destroyer and the father of lies, destroyed a Christian family—mine—and he almost destroyed me. Like my home of origin, my mind became a battlefield for Christ and Satan. Satan planted his lies, I believed them, and I became depressed . . . to the point where death seemed like the only escape.

But this was Satan's biggest lie yet. And that mindset toward self-destruction was just a counterfeit identity from the thief who comes only "to steal and kill and destroy" (John 10:10). It is the same mindset Satan plants in millions who take their own lives—it is the mindset he must have planted in the mind of a girl I grew up with who, tragically, took her own life just as I was preparing this manuscript for publication.

Sadly, the negative thoughts in a depressed mind become so familiar that victims think they are embedded into their DNA. They think these thoughts are merely *who they are,* and they believe that their constant misery cannot be destroyed unless *they* are destroyed. But what a lie! What a tragedy not to see that it is Satan directing their thoughts, and their steps, and not to realize that they can uproot those thoughts and have a new mind, before it is too late.

That's why I have been so honest in exposing my struggles and telling my story. Only when we expose Satan's lies can we fight them. On the other hand, if we don't recognize what Satan is doing behind the scenes, we are in big trouble! As Ellen White puts it: "None are in greater danger from the influence of evil spirits than those who . . . deny the existence and agency of the devil and his angels. So long as we are ignorant of their wiles, they have almost inconceivable advantage; many give heed to their suggestions while they suppose themselves to be following the dictates of their own wisdom. . . . It is [Satan's] policy to conceal himself and his manner of working."[1]

Yes, Satan is good at concealing himself and his lies. But God—when we ask God to help us—is even better at revealing His truth. I hope this book has helped you to have faith in God, and to have hope that, *with God,* life can get better. I hope you have seen how God readily and overwhelmingly responds when we cry out to Him. And while it's true that we might not feel a big difference right away (I certainly didn't—depression recovery sometimes happens slowly, similar to maturing into adulthood and/or developing a mature faith), I encourage you not to give up.

Keep praying and keep reading the Bible, or start, if you haven't (I suggest starting with the recommended reading and sample prayers in the back of this book). Choose music, books, friends, and environments that encourage you to seek God. If you are currently in a desperate situation, tell somebody; get help. If you have come from a stressful or traumatic background with unresolved pain, honor your losses in prayer, and then with some trusted friends if you have them, or a Christian counselor. If nothing else has helped, perhaps medication is necessary—and for some, it is a great blessing—but I believe it should be a last resort. (As Buc always tells me, I didn't need medication as much as I just needed some good listeners and some prayer.) Finally, shun those negative influences that point you away from God and to the world. Most of all, reject those negative thoughts in your mind telling you that *you are worthless* and *life is hopeless,* because those are lies, and as long as you believe them, Satan will have victory in your life (you can find a list of more negative thoughts in the back of this book).

At the end of our journey together, I hope you see a surefire cure to depression, if not a "quick fix": it is to uproot Satan's lies and replace them with God's truth (in addition to medication and other lifestyle changes, for those who respond). If you will accept that the "root" of depression is spiritual warfare—and that it is not really about us, but about Christ versus Satan *in our minds*—then I am convinced you have a great chance of recovery—and until recovery, hope—because Christ has already overcome Satan.

That is the truth, and that is why I can confidently and happily tell my story.

Acknowledgments

It is with deep humility that I write this section of my book, the very last, after many manuscript drafts. I wanted to write a book several years ago, but God knew I wasn't ready to write the book He wanted me to write. He had to humble me before I could write these words. And I'm glad for the process. It reminds me that my Christian development is not finished yet. Like this book manuscript, I always need revision. I need searching inside my own heart. I need prayer for God to take over. I need the insight of trusted friends and counselors to redirect my fragments and bad ideas. And I need encouragement when I want to quit. Here's to the many counselors who helped bring this work to a fruitful conclusion.

My heartfelt thanks to Paul Coneff, who broke the Bread of Life to me in a fresh way through his message, *The Hidden Half of the Gospel*. Without your prayer ministry and discipleship, I might still be spinning my wheels in graduate school, trying to find my next steps—and a conclusion for this manuscript. Praying with you and co-writing your book taught me that I could trust God enough to lay down my fear-based career ambitions and write, and more than that, become a mom!

I want to especially thank my older brother, Kyle, who has been a beacon of faith to me through the years (after we got past our days of sibling fights!). You know what I went through growing up because you went through it too, and your life of serving Jesus has continually inspired me.

Buc, my white knight, you have been with me through the nitty-gritty of spiritual rebirth and recovery from depression over the past ten years. You have seen tears and tantrums (sorry again for that shoe incident) that no one else has seen as I've gone through the changes mentioned, but not fully described, in this book. And you still love me. Wow. I thank you for always believing in my writing and making me believe it should be shared with the world. Your love has been such a gift to me. I can't imagine life without you! Thanks again for inviting me to come to Texas to share my life with you.

Samantha, our matchmaker and my best friend—how dear our friendship is to me! Like Buc, you have seen some not-so-pretty parts of me that no one else has seen. We both moved our lives from Minnesota to Texas and have moved through life together; not everyone gets a friend like that, but I am so grateful God gave me you!

There are a handful of friends and family who read the first and worst draft of this manuscript, and I can't tell you how healing it was to have you read those pages. Aunt Cheri, Tasha, Manda, Nicole, and cousin Michelle—you gave me the gift of being able to share my story before I could put it into sensible chronology and pretty words, and I needed that gift. I needed people just to cry with me at first. Thank you.

My Texas writers group, Project Memoir, especially Lea Weaver and Laurie Lindemeier: you provided an objective audience to push me to describe my early faith story so non-Adventists, and non-Christians, could understand. I am so glad I got to work with fellow memory makers; what fun it was!

Jim Warren, my thesis advisor—your instruction on the teaching of writing was the best thing about graduate school. Because of you, I will always consider my audience, and teach my students to do the same.

Author Trish Ryan, what a highlight it was to have your input on this manuscript! Before I worked with you, you provided one of my first examples of a well-written Christian memoir, *He Loves Me, He Loves Me Not*, which I have since reread and enthusiastically shared with others. Thanks for seeing the potential in my soggy (crying) scenes and confused chronology and pushing me to dig deep for the scenes that set the stage for my real story of new life in Christ.

Fellow bloggers, especially Luanne, Kate, Cinda, and Vinidhini, thanks for giving me your time, prayers, and encouragement during the first years of *Writing to My Roots*. Your comments always encourage me and push me to keep writing for an audience.

My sisters in Christ, friends, and prayer partners from the Straight 2 the Heart prayer groups mentioned in this book: Amanda, Mary, Ashley, Christina, Julie, Susan, Eugenia, Linda, Devon, Tammy, and the women from the Grandview church. How I cherish the friendships we built as we brought our hurts and hearts to one another at the foot of the Cross. Praying with you and hearing your stories made me realize how we all have painful stories, and how important it is to share them so we can "bear one another's burdens." Through the telling, healing comes.

Lastly, my families:

My Texas family, the Gendkes: Mike, Margie, Bo, Deborah, Brady, Joanna, Madi, Megan, Taylor, Emma, and Max. I kind of lumped you together in this story as a unit—a big, loud, loving, Italian unit—and that's a compliment. You showed me much about family unity—how families should stick together and do things together and spend lots of time together and hug a whole lot (Margie, I guess you stick out with the hugging; but I mean that as a compliment, too!). I'm so glad to have you, all of you! Special thanks to Margie and Auntie Joanna ("Tia") for the babysitting time that allowed me to get this manuscript closer to its final product.

And my Minnesota family, Mom, Dad, Kyle, and Caleb: thanks for allowing me to publish this secret story of ours in the name of the "bigger picture," which is no less than the great controversy. I know this story is not the one you wanted or planned for our family; but today I am glad for it, and I hope you can be glad also. Without this story, none of us would know God the way we know Him today—and I believe it will lead other hearts to know God more deeply too. Let's continue to grow up in Him, letting our roots go deep in Christ (Colossians 2:6, 7; Ephesians 3:18, 19). Special thanks to Mom for praying and crying with me through this manuscript (several times), and for your wise and insightful feedback.

Lastly, my Lord and Savior, Jesus Christ. Without Your story, mine would be a mess. Thank You for suffering for me and saving my life in so many ways. I can't wait for the day when I can thank You in person.

Questions for Discussion

1. What misunderstandings about God did Lindsey have growing up, and what do you think caused these misunderstandings?
2. What changes in Lindsey's home environment or schooling might have helped her to understand the Sabbath in a positive light?
3. Using examples from the book, discuss why it's important for parents to be grounded in the faith in which they are raising their children.
4. What were the elephants in Lindsey's home? How do you think these contributed to what happened? How could they have been prevented?
5. If your family had gone through a situation like Lindsey's, how might they have handled it? What do you think would be the *best* way to handle a situation like this?
6. What factors contributed to Lindsey's depression? When do you think her depression first started?
7. Compare and contrast Lindsey's behavior before leaving her parents: first, the scene of leaving her dad (chapter 8), and then, the scene of leaving her mom (chapter 10). What do you think these scenes say about the importance of parental involvement even in the late high school years and beyond?
8. What role do boys and boyfriends play in Lindsey's story? How do you explain the poor choices Lindsey made in this area (before she met Buc)?
9. Why did Lindsey have so much trouble fitting into her new family and her new church in Texas? Have you ever had a similar struggle?
10. Discuss Kyle's role in the book. What changes does he personally undergo, and how does his relationship with Lindsey change over the course of the book?
11. Why do you think Lindsey's teaching stint was so life-changing? In the context of depression recovery, what is so important about starting and holding down a career?
12. Discuss the foremost habit Lindsey formed during her second year of teaching. How did this help in her battle with depression?
13. In the last third of the book, what did Lindsey discover she still had not healed from? What new understanding did she receive from "The Hidden Half of the Gospel" message, and in what new ways did she heal through prayer ministry?

14. Compare and contrast the ways in which the college retreat preacher (chapter 1) and Pastor Paul Coneff (chapter 22) presented the gospel. What was the difference, in both delivery and in message? Which do you think is the more effective method?

15. What were some natural results of Lindsey's healing in the final chapters of the book?

16. Think back to your experiences in church, at presentations of the gospel, evangelistic seminars, or other discipleship programs. Do you feel like they adequately addressed the real problems that Christians and non-Christians struggle with? If not, what could you and your church do to meet people in the middle of these struggles?

17. Do you agree with Lindsey that honesty about our sins and struggles is a necessary part of healing? Are there any exceptions, or contexts in which full disclosure is not appropriate? Does the idea of being honest with an audience, as Lindsey was with her prayer group and on her blog, encourage you or scare you? Why?

18. As you read, did you relate to any of Lindsey's negative self-talk, or the lies and negative roots Satan had planted in her? If so, can you see how Jesus suffered or was tempted like you? Feel free to use the attached worksheets and sample prayers to begin connecting your story to Jesus' story.

Additional Resources

Satan's Lies in My Life (Worksheet A)

What negative thoughts or messages have I received because of painful relationships, experiences, losses, or sinful behaviors in my life? (Jesus taught that these thoughts come from Satan, "the father of lies" [John 8:44].)

- ❑ I'm rejected
- ❑ I have no hope
- ❑ Poor me/why me
- ❑ I can't trust others
- ❑ I'm powerless/helpless
- ❑ I'm alone/I'm abandoned
- ❑ I'm not worthy/I'm worthless
- ❑ I have to do more and try harder
- ❑ I never get to have my needs met
- ❑ Something bad is going to happen
- ❑ It's my fault/I'm not good enough
- ❑ I'll never be loved, wanted, valued
- ❑ I can't speak up or share my needs
- ❑ I'm not safe/I have to protect myself
- ❑ I don't have a right to protect myself
- ❑ I have to be in control/control others
- ❑ I have to look good in front of others
- ❑ I've got to defend myself (image control)
- ❑ I can't trust or rely on anyone but myself
- ❑ I'm bad/I should have been better/I hate myself
- ❑ I can't be forgiven/accepted—I have to live with guilt

How Jesus Can Identify With Me (Worksheet B)

Where was Jesus *tempted* to believe the same negative thoughts that Satan tempts me to believe? (Hebrews 2:14–18; 4:14–16)

- ❏ Born to an unwed mother (Luke 2:5)
- ❏ Rejected by those He loved (Matthew 23:37; John 7:3, 5)
- ❏ Abandoned by those closest to Him in His time of need
- ❏ Struggled to surrender His will to His Father
- ❏ Betrayed, denied, and lied about by His closest friends (Luke 22:47, 48, 54–62)
- ❏ Stripped naked (Matthew 27:27, 28)
- ❏ Physically violated (Matthew 27:29–31)
- ❏ Shamed and humiliated
- ❏ Mocked, spit on, and blamed
- ❏ The object of racial, religious, and political prejudice by men in power over Him who should have been protecting Him
- ❏ Tempted to numb His pain
- ❏ Tempted to believe His situation was hopeless and useless
- ❏ Cried out to His Father, "Why have You forsaken Me?" in His deepest, darkest moments
- ❏ Not seen, heard, valued, understood, appreciated, or respected
- ❏ Not safe
- ❏ Unjustly accused, convicted, and murdered

After you have identified your negative thoughts (A) and where Jesus identifies with you (B), transfer this information to the next page and pray the sample prayer.

Used with permission from Paul and Cristina Coneff, www.straight2theheart.com and www.hiddenhalf.org.

Connecting My Story to Jesus' Story (Sample Prayer)[2]

(A) Dear Lord Jesus, thank You for choosing to fulfill prophecy, going through the same experiences I have: _____

_____

_____

_____

(B) Thank You for suffering in Your soul, dying for me, taking to death all the ways I've been wounded in life, and the ways I've trusted in my own strength to provide for myself, protect myself, and prove who I am. Thank You for healing my wounded heart and setting me free from: _____

_____

_____

_____ as I receive my truest, deepest identity as (Your son *or* Your daughter) through Your resurrection power, **in Your name, Jesus, amen.**

(C) Blessing/Barrier Prayer: Dear Jesus, do You have any blessings, truth, or words of encouragement—or do You want to reveal any negative thoughts keeping me from receiving Your freedom in this area of my life? _____

_____

_____

Warfare Prayer: Dear Jesus, how will Satan tempt me to cooperate with his lies, keeping me from receiving Your forgiveness, freedom, and protection this week? And what protection do You have for me?

(D) Satan's attacks _____

(E) God's protection _____

Use as many copies of this page as needed. Expand on these themes by using the daily prayers on the next page.

Used with permission from Paul and Cristina Coneff, www.straight2theheart.com and www.hiddenhalf.org.

Daily Prayers

These are the same daily prayers I describe in chapter 22 as I "Learned to Pray."

Day 1: (A) Dear Lord Jesus, is there a place where You can connect more of Your story with my story of being _____
_____? (Isaiah 53; 50:4, 5; 61:1–3; Matthew 26–28; Luke 22–24; other gospel stories, etc.)

Day 2: (B) Dear Lord Jesus, is there anything more You want to reveal to me about my losses and lies keeping me from receiving the fullness of Your freedom? (Anything more about being unseen, unheard, abandoned, betrayed, abused, falsely accused/lied about, rejected, invalidated, or violated?) (Psalms 109:4, 5, 21, 22; 86:11, 12; 139:23, 24)

Day 3: (B) Dear Lord Jesus, is there anything else You want to reveal to me about the ways I've learned to trust in my own strength and my own will power to protect myself, provide for myself, and/or prove who I am? (Luke 4:4–13; Psalms 51:6–10; 139:23, 24; Matthew 15:18, 19; 2 Peter 1:5–11)

Day 4: (C) Dear Lord Jesus, are there any other blessings You have for me in this area of my life? (Scripture promises, songs, characteristics, encouragement; see Ephesians 1:3–10; Galatians 5:22, 23)

Day 5: (D) Dear Lord Jesus, are there other ways Satan will tempt me to cooperate with his lies so he can keep me from receiving Your healing and freedom? (John 10:10; Matthew 12:43–45; Hebrews 3:12; Luke 4:18–20; Ephesians 6:10–12)

Day 6: (E) Dear Lord Jesus, are there any other ways You want to offer me Your protection from these attacks, and any ways I can thank You and praise You? (John 17:10, 11; Psalm 23; Colossians 2:15; 1 Thessalonians 5:16–18; Revelation 5:5; Ephesians 6:10–18)

Day 7: Dear Lord Jesus, is there anything else You want me to know about my losses and lies that will help me to receive Your victory over all of Satan's attacks against me? (Matthew 28:18–20; Colossians 2:6–15)

Used with permission from Paul and Cristina Coneff, www.straight2theheart.com and www.hiddenhalf.org.

Recommended Reading

If you were blessed by *Ending the Pain,* I recommend:

The Hidden Half of the Gospel: How His Suffering Can Heal Yours, by Paul Coneff[1] with Lindsey Gendke www.hiddenhalf.org. Here you can read more about the message that changed my life, including how to identify your negative roots, and how Jesus can relate to your story. Included is my testimony, along with the testimonies of many others who have applied this message to their stories of betrayal, abuse, addiction, rejection, and more.

Straight 2 the Heart prayer ministry www.straight2theheart.com. If you are interested in learning more about the prayer ministry that I describe in Part 3 of this book, you can find more information at this website. Here you can also find information on contacting Paul Coneff or scheduling him to visit your church.

My Web site and blog, *Writing to My Roots* www.lindseygendke.com. Here I write about everything from my recovery from depression to how I am adapting to motherhood to my daily journey of faith.

The Bible, in a version that is easy for you to read and understand (I like the New Living Translation). If you're new to the Bible, I suggest starting with the Gospels, Matthew, Mark, Luke, and John, so you can get the "heart" of the Bible, or Jesus' story. If you are dealing with depression, I also highly recommend the Psalms and Paul's epistles, especially Ephesians and Philippians. You will be best served by the Bible if you also commit to memorizing key verses. (Refer to my chapter 19, "Rebirth," for ideas on how I did it, and for some of the scriptures that most encouraged me.)

The Great Controversy, by Ellen G. White. While my memoir depicted Satan's lies battling God's truth at the "micro" level—in one heart and in one family—Mrs. White gives the much broader picture of how Satan has tried, and is trying, to sabotage Christianity through the ages with his lies. For those unfamiliar with the Seventh-day Adventist faith, she also delineates our core beliefs and how issues such as the Sabbath will play a special part in the end-time great controversy between Christ and Satan.

---

1. Paul Coneff, who trained me to facilitate prayer and who created this sample prayer, always asks if the person receiving prayer prefers to pray to Jesus or the Father (either is great). Some people are uncomfortable with praying to Jesus, but Paul (Coneff) explains that in the Bible, Stephen, Paul, Ananias, and Peter all prayed to Jesus or had direct communication with Him *after* His resurrection, ascension, and upper room experience (Acts 7:55–60; 9:5, 17; 10:14, 36). In addition, Jesus also said that His sheep "hear His voice" multiple times in John 10.
2. Ellen G. White, *The Great Controversy* (Nampa, ID: Pacific Press® Publishing Association, 2005), 516.